FUELING UP

The Economic Implications of America's Oil and Gas Boom

FUELING UP

The Economic Implications of America's Oil and Gas Boom

Trevor Houser and Shashank Mohan

PETERSON INSTITUTE FOR INTERNATIONAL ECONOMICS

WASHINGTON, DC
JANUARY 2014

Trevor Houser, visiting fellow at the Peterson Institute for International Economics, is partner at the Rhodium Group, where he leads the firm's energy and natural resources work. He is also an adjunct lecturer at the City College of New York and a visiting fellow at the school's Colin Powell Center for Policy Studies. He is a member of the Council on Foreign Relations and the National Committee on US-China Relations and serves on the Advisory Board of Asia Society's Center on US-China Relations. He speaks regularly on international energy market and policy trends and has testified before the House Energy and Commerce Committee, the House Select Committee on Energy Independence and Global Warming, the US Helsinki Commission, and the US-China Economic and Security Review Commissions. During 2009, he served as senior advisor to the US State Department, where he worked on a broad range of international energy and environmental policy issues. His areas of research include energy, commodity and environmental policy and markets, and energy-related international trade and investment issues. He is coauthor of *Leveling the Carbon Playing Field: International Competition and US Climate Policy Design* (2008) and *China Energy: A Guide for the Perplexed* (2007).

Shashank Mohan is a director at the Rhodium Group (RHG), where he leads the development and management of the company's suite of economic models and other quantitative tools. He works across RHG practice areas to analyze the impact of policy proposals and structural developments on specific markets and broader economic trends. Prior to RHG, he worked with Columbia University's Earth Institute and the World Bank to design an electricity expansion model for Kenya and Senegal and was a program assistant at the South Asia Institute. His background is in information technology, with a previous career in software engineering at Microsoft. He holds an MPA from the School of International and Public Affairs at Columbia University and is a graduate of the Indian Institute of Technology (IIT), Kharagpur.

PETERSON INSTITUTE FOR
INTERNATIONAL ECONOMICS
1750 Massachusetts Avenue, NW
Washington, DC 20036-1903
(202) 328-9000   FAX: (202) 659-3225
www.piie.com

Adam S. Posen, *President*
Steven R. Weisman, *Editorial and Publications Director*

Graphics typesetted by BMWW
Cover design by Fletcher Design
Cover photo by Ralf Hettler
Printing by Versa Press, Inc.

Printed in the United States of America
16   15   14   5   4   3   2   1

Library of Congress Cataloging-in-Publication Data
Houser, Trevor.
  Fueling up : the economic implications of America's oil and gas boom / Trevor Houser and Shashank Mohan.
    pages cm
  ISBN 978-0-88132-656-7
  1. Petroleum industry and trade—United States. 2. Gas industry—United States. 3. Energy consumption—United States. 4. Energy policy—United States. I. Mohan, Shashank. II. Title.
  HD9565.H68 2013
  338.2'7280973--dc23
                                    2013036645

This publication has been subjected to a prepublication peer review intended to ensure analytical quality. The views expressed are those of the authors. This publication is part of the overall program of the Peterson Institute for International Economics, as endorsed by its Board of Directors, but it does not necessarily reflect the views of individual members of the Board or of the Institute's staff or management. The Institute is an independent, private, nonprofit institution for rigorous, intellectually honest study and open discussion of international economic policy. Its work is made possible by financial support from a highly diverse group of philanthropic foundations, private corporations, and interested individuals, as well as by income on its capital fund. For a list of Institute supporters, please see www.piie.com/supporters.cfm.

For

Kurt M. Pickett (1972–2011)

&

Renu Agarwal and family

Contents

Tables

Figures

Preface

The United States is in the midst of an energy production renaissance. Using new drilling techniques, American companies are extracting oil and natural gas from previously inaccessible reservoirs, and at an astounding pace. Natural gas output grew by 25 percent between 2007 and 2012, making the United States the largest natural gas producer in the world. US crude oil production grew by 28 percent, accounting for more than half of the growth in global supply over that period.

With the United States still struggling to emerge from the Great Recession, many are looking to the current oil and gas boom as a potential source of economic salvation. In North Dakota and a handful of other energy-rich states, oil and gas investment has helped drive unemployment rates back down to prerecession levels. Lower natural gas prices have increased households' spending power and are making some energy-intensive domestic industries more competitive. And America's energy trade deficit is falling sharply.

Despite the attention the US oil and gas boom has received, however, there has been little objective analysis of its economic consequences. In this important study, Trevor Houser and Shashank Mohan shed light on whether an oil and gas production surge in the United States can lead to a manufacturing renaissance and broader US economic revival. Their main conclusion is that over the next few years, with a lot of available labor supply, the boom will act as a potent economic stimulus: It will increase investment demand in the energy and related sectors with an increase in household spending thanks to lower energy costs. Between 2013 and 2020, they estimate that the oil and gas boom could increase annual GDP growth by as much as 0.2 percent, for a cumulative 2.1 percent increase in economic output. This is not enough to bring about an early recovery, but that would be a substantial ongoing contribution to US economic growth. Employment effects are similarly beneficial but modest.

The long-term economic benefits are likely to be more modest, however. In line with standard economics, Houser and Mohan find that as the economy returns to full employment, any investment and job creation in oil and gas production and supporting industries would increasingly come at the expense of other sectors. While the boom would transform a handful of specific industries and regional economies, those looking for an energy-driven broad-based economic renaissance will be disappointed. That is due to the size and diversity of the US economy. For example, while lower-cost natural gas is improving the competitiveness of some forms of energy-intensive manufacturing, these industries account for only a small share of manufacturing employment, which in turn is a sixth or less of overall US employment. And all else being equal, a declining energy trade deficit should put upward pressure on the US dollar, which could erode the competitiveness of other manufacturing industries where energy input costs are less important (like automobiles, electronics, and aviation).

Given that future levels of domestic oil and gas production are inherently unknown, Houser and Mohan assess the economic impact of both a pessimistic and an optimistic production outlook to capture the range of current private- and public-sector supply forecasts. They analyze the impact of these scenarios on energy prices, investment, economic growth, manufacturing competitiveness, and job creation between now and 2035.

After more than two decades of declining domestic oil and gas production, Houser and Mohan say that the surprise boom in supply is remaking the energy landscape, both in the United States and abroad, even if the overall macroeconomic effects are far less profound. Domestic natural gas prices have fallen dramatically, saving businesses and households money and providing a low-cost (and cleaner) alternative to coal as fuel for electric power generation. US natural gas imports have plummeted, shaking up global gas markets and putting downward pressure on gas prices in other parts of the world. Rising domestic crude production has mitigated the oil price impact of Western sanctions against Iran and political unrest in the Middle East and North Africa. US crude oil imports are declining and the country is now a net exporter of refined petroleum products.

The Houser-Mohan study also analyzes some important environmental and trade policy implications of rising oil and gas production. Environmental groups are increasingly wary of environmental consequences both local and global of the exploration, extraction, production, and use of these new energy supplies. They argue that these risks can be successfully managed and that there are important environmental benefits to be had from increased natural gas consumption. America's rapidly changing energy trade position also raises a new front for the battles over US export restrictions. Some contend that allowing energy exports would erode the country's new-found energy cost advantage or even undermine national security. Houser and Mohan see no evidence that open international energy trade—including US gas and oil exports—would undermine the domestic benefits of the oil and gas boom.

The Peterson Institute for International Economics is a private, nonprofit institution for rigorous, intellectually open, and honest study and discussion of international economic policy. Its purpose is to identify and analyze important issues to making globalization beneficial and sustainable for the people of the United States and the world and then to develop and communicate practical new approaches for dealing with them. The Institute is completely nonpartisan.

The Institute's work is funded by a highly diverse group of philanthropic foundations, private corporations, and interested individuals, as well as by income on its capital fund. About 35 percent of the Institute's resources in our latest fiscal year were provided by contributors from outside the United States. BP America, Cheniere Energy, Chevron Corporation, and Dow Chemical Company provided generous support for this study. For a list of Institute supporters, see www.piie.com/supporters.cfm.

The Executive Committee of the Institute's Board of Directors bears overall responsibility for the Institute's direction, gives general guidance and approval to its research program, and evaluates its performance in pursuit of its mission. The Institute's President is responsible for the identification of topics that are likely to become important over the medium term (one to three years) that should be addressed by Institute scholars. This rolling agenda is set in close consultation with the Institute's research staff and Board of Directors, as well as other stakeholders.

The President makes the final decision to publish any individual Institute study, following independent internal and external review of the work.

The Institute hopes that its research and other activities will contribute to building a stronger foundation for international economic policy around the world. We invite readers of these publications to let us know how they think we can best accomplish this objective.

ADAM S. POSEN
President
January 2014

Acknowledgments

This book benefited enormously from an extensive peer review process led by Marcus Noland of the Peterson Institute of International Economics. We thank Daniel Ahn, C. Fred Bergsten, Jason Bordoff, William Cline, Charles Ebinger, Mark Finley, Steven Friis, Joseph Gagnon, Gary Hufbauer, Jan Kalicki, Barbara Kotschwar, Sara Ladislaw, Frank Loy, Michael Levi, David Pumphrey, Jeffrey Schott, Phil Sharp, Arvind Subramanian, Frank Verrastro, Andrew Ware, John Williamson, and an anonymous reviewer for their invaluable input and review comments.

For production and organizational support we thank Steve Weisman, Madona Devasahayam, Susann Luetjen, and particularly Ed Tureen of the Peterson Institute, who recently passed away. Ed, you will be greatly, greatly missed.

We are grateful for the incredible support and guidance we received throughout this project from our families and colleagues at the Rhodium Group.

We wish to acknowledge BP America, Cheniere Energy, Chevron Corporation, and Dow Chemical Company for their generous support of this study.

TREVOR HOUSER
SHASHANK MOHAN

1

Introduction

Keeping America competitive requires affordable energy. And here we have a serious problem: America is addicted to oil, which is often imported from unstable parts of the world.... By applying the talent and technology of America, this country can dramatically improve our environment, move beyond a petroleum-based economy, and make our dependence on Middle Eastern oil a thing of the past.

—President George W. Bush

When President George W. Bush called for an end to US oil dependence in his 2006 State of the Union address, American businesses and consumers were experiencing a surge in petroleum prices not witnessed since the late 1970s. The cost of crude oil had doubled since President Bush took office and gasoline prices were up by nearly 40 percent. Domestic oil production had been declining for decades while demand continued to grow, leaving the United States dependent on imports for 60 percent of its oil supply. In the wake of the September 11 terrorist attacks, Americans had grown increasingly anxious about their country's reliance on foreign oil and its implications for US foreign policy, national security, and economic vitality. And there was no relief in sight.

The Energy Information Administration (EIA 2006) projected a continued decline in US crude oil production, from 5.8 million barrels per day (bbl/d) in 2000 to 4.6 million bbl/d by 2030, and a 40 percent increase in demand over the same period. US oil imports would exceed 17 million bbl/d by 2030, more than total US oil demand during the 1980s and early 1990s. Moreover, it looked like those imports would be coming from increasingly unstable parts of the world. Sixty-two percent of the world's proven oil reserves were in the Middle East and 75 percent of global reserves were controlled by the Organization of Petroleum Exporting Countries (OPEC) (BP 2006). Against this backdrop, President Bush, himself a former oil man from Texas, called for the United States to start abandoning oil as an energy source, stressing that the only way to safeguard the US economy and American national security was to reduce demand through efficiency and develop alternative sources of supply. He called for increased funding for electric vehicle research and greater use of ethanol as a transportation fuel. In 2007 he worked with a Democratic Congress to pass the Energy Independence and Security Act, which raised vehicle efficiency standards and established a biofuels mandate.

While oil received the most attention, high natural gas costs were exacting a significant toll on the US economy as well. Natural gas prices rose alongside crude oil prices, from less than $3 per cubic foot during the 1990s (in 2012 dollars) to $8 per cubic foot by July 2005. Hurricanes Katrina and Rita took out significant quantities of natural gas production in the Gulf of Mexico in August and September, and prices spiked above $15. Businesses and households saw an increase not only in natural gas costs but also in their electricity bills, as natural gas sets the marginal power price in many parts of the country. With natural gas production expected to remain flat through 2030, most analysts expected the United States would increasingly rely on imported and relatively expensive liquefied natural gas (LNG) to meet growing demand.

What a difference six years made. Through technological advances such as horizontal drilling and hydraulic fracturing (fracking), the oil and gas industry began to extract large quantities of natural gas from previously inaccessible shale formations. The rise in natural gas prices between 2000 and 2006 attracted the investment required to deploy these technologies at scale. When President Barack Obama gave his State of the Union address in January 2012, US natural gas production was 30 percent higher than it was during President Bush's speech in 2006. Thanks to this abundant supply, prices were nearly 70 percent lower. LNG terminals built to import natural gas began to be overhauled to export gas instead. The US chemicals industry was increasingly profitable and competitive thanks to low-cost feedstock. Though Obama had come into office pledging to move the country away from fossil fuels, he extolled the economic benefits of natural gas in his 2012 and 2013 State of the Union speeches.

The fracking process used to extract natural gas from shale can be used to produce oil as well. As natural gas prices have fallen thanks to new unconventional supply and oil prices have risen due to robust demand in Asia and instability in the Middle East and North Africa, US oil and gas companies have shifted focus to tight oil—the crude produced from unconventional reservoirs in North Dakota, Texas, and other parts of the country. American tight oil output has grown by 1.5 million barrels per day since 2006, reversing a quarter-century decline in US oil production (EIA 2013a). High oil prices also have made deepwater exploration in the Gulf of Mexico more economically attractive. US offshore production rose by 400,000 barrels per day between 2006 and the beginning of 2010. While the Deepwater Horizon oil spill reversed most of those gains, the prospects for continued growth in offshore production in the years ahead are bright if high oil prices persist. Oil companies are even exploring other previously inaccessible or uneconomic resources, such as offshore production in the Arctic and oil shale deposits in the Rocky Mountains.

By the end of 2012, net imports as a share of US oil consumption had fallen below 40 percent—levels not seen since the early 1990s. This growth in production has led many observers to proclaim the dawn of a US oil and gas renaissance (Morse et al. 2012, Adkins and Molchanov 2012, Verleger 2012).[1] In this view of the future, reduced oil imports and cheap natural gas will revolutionize US foreign policy and revitalize domestic manufacturing. The United States could even become energy independent within a decade, a goal most analysts and policymakers long considered impossible. More skeptical observers question the ability of the oil and gas industry to keep production growing at its current pace or warn that even if the optimists' supply outlook is correct, it will not have as great an effect on US national security or the economy as they think (Brackett 2012, Securing America's Future Energy 2012, Trivedi et al. 2012).[2,3]

Producers and consumers have already begun battling over the emerging energy future. Faced with historically low domestic natural prices and historically high prices in other parts of the world, US companies are looking to export low-cost US supply. Gas-dependent residential and industrial consumers are concerned that linking the United States to international markets could erase nascent shale-driven energy savings.[4] The recent fight over whether the government should approve LNG export terminals could be the first act in a new trade policy drama. With net US oil imports rapidly declining, a battle over America's prohibition on crude oil exports is next in line.

Environmental groups are growing increasingly wary of the US oil and gas boom and many are actively working to stop it.[5] The impact of shale gas and tight oil production on local air and water quality is their primary concern. Fracking involves injecting water and chemicals into a well to coax oil or natural gas out of reservoirs with low permeability. Opponents worry that the fluids from fracking could leak into ground water supplies or be improperly disposed of once recovered from the well. Emissions from trucks and drilling

---

1. See also John Deutch, "The US Natural-Gas Boom Will Transform the World," *Wall Street Journal*, August 14, 2012, http://professional.wsj.com/article/SB10001424052702303343404577514622469426012.html?mod=rss_opinion_main&wpisrc=nl_wonk&mg=reno64-wsj (accessed on September 8, 2013); David Ignatius, "An Economic Boom Ahead?" *Washington Post*, May 6, 2012, www.washingtonpost.com/opinions/an-economic-boom-ahead/2012/05/04/gIQAbj5K2T_story.html (accessed on September 8, 2013).

2. See also Kate Mackenzie, "Shale Oil Everywhere... for a While," *Financial Times*, August 13, 2012, http://ftalphaville.ft.com/2012/08/13/1101721/shale-oil-everywhere-for-a-while (accessed on September 8, 2013); Ian Urbina, "Insiders Sound an Alarm Amid a Natural Gas Rush," *New York Times*, June 25, 2011, www.nytimes.com/2011/06/26/us/26gas.html?_r=1 (accessed on September 8, 2013); and Chris Nelder, "The Murky Future of U.S. Shale Gas," *SmartPlanet*, October 17, 2012, www.smartplanet.com/blog/take/the-murky-future-of-us-shale-gas/157 (accessed on September 8, 2013).

3. For excellent and independent discussions of the competing visions of America's energy futures, see Levi (2013), Ladislaw et al. (2013), and Bordoff (2013).

4. Amy Harder, "Democratic Gas Blockade," *National Journal*, July 18, 2012.

5. Amy Harder, "Chamber, Sierra Club Wage Dueling Shale-Gas Campaigns," *National Journal*, July 26, 2012.

rigs used in shale development can also adversely affect air quality and respiratory health. Fracking has even been linked to increased earthquake activity. Following the Deepwater Horizon spill, the environmental community is likewise skeptical of the industry's ability to produce challenging offshore oil and gas resources safely, whether in the Gulf of Mexico or the Alaskan Arctic. There is a broad sense of unease that emerging oil and gas resources will lower fossil fuel prices, making it harder for renewables to compete and complicating efforts to reduce US carbon dioxide emissions to combat climate change. Reports that shale gas wells leak large quantities of methane, another greenhouse gas, make environmental groups that much more worried.

Government and private sector forecasters have started to assess the effect of a US oil and gas renaissance on the country's energy future. But analysis of the economic and environmental consequences has been more limited, either driven by interest groups or focusing on a particular industry or issue. This book attempts to assess the situation more comprehensively to help readers navigate the debate. In chapter 2 we discuss the economic cost of rising oil and gas prices between 2002 and 2008 and the fears of energy shortage it created. Chapter 3 describes the emerging energy renaissance that proponents argue will provide much-needed economic relief and evaluates the range of current oil and gas supply projections. We model the economic and employment effects of these projections and discuss our findings in chapter 4. In chapter 5 we turn to the demand side of the energy equation, where efficiency improvements are working alongside the growth in supply to reduce US dependence on imported energy. Chapter 6 analyzes the distributional effects of America's changing energy landscape—which states and industries have the most to gain, and to lose. In chapter 7 we assess the environmental costs and benefits of increased US oil and gas supply. Chapter 8 discusses trade policy implications. We conclude with recommendations for policymakers on how to respond to America's rapidly changing energy future.

2

The Dark before the Dawn

The potential economic benefits of the current oil and gas boom can be understood only in the context of the economic cost of rising oil and gas prices that prompted President George W. Bush's 2006 State of the Union address and the specter of the price spikes that preceded it. In October 1973, after more than a decade of rapid growth in oil demand that left the United States increasingly dependent on imports, the Yom Kippur War led to an abrupt disruption in Middle East supply (Yergin 1991). Prices, which had been held in check for decades by spare US production capacity and the Texas Railroad Commission, tripled over the course of a year. In the view of many scholars, this was a leading cause of the 1973–74 economic recession (Hamilton 2009a). Shortly after the war broke out, President Richard Nixon called for an aggressive program of energy efficiency and the development of alternative sources of supply to help the country achieve energy "self-sufficiency."[1] Six years later, net US energy imports had risen from 17 to 21 percent (EIA 2012b), the Iranian revolution had pushed oil prices up even higher, and the economy fell into recession again in January 1980. This time it was President Jimmy Carter's turn to sound the energy alarm. In a speech in July 1979, Carter called for cutting US oil imports in half by 1990 and pushed further to develop oil alternatives and conservation strategies to help achieve that goal.

By 1982 the tide had started to turn. US dependence on imported oil fell modestly as the new Trans-Alaska Pipeline brought oil from Alaska's North Slope to the lower 48 states. Power plants switched from oil to coal thanks to both high oil prices and government encouragement. Oil demand growth in the transportation sector slowed as drivers opted for more fuel-efficient vehi-

---

1. Richard Nixon, Address to the Nation about National Energy Policy, November 25, 1973.

cles. Oil imports started rising again in 1986, but prices stayed low for another decade and a half thanks to slower global demand growth and increased oil supply from the North Sea, Mexico, and other parts of the world.

As panic about the adequacy of oil and gas supply abated, President Ronald Reagan slashed funding for federal programs focused on developing alternatives. Consumer demand for more energy-efficient vehicles ground to a halt, as did government efforts to raise fuel economy standards. For most Americans, energy was no longer a concern. Then, in the early 2000s, prices started to rise. The cost of crude oil to US refineries rose from $31 per barrel in 2002 (in real 2012 dollars) to more than $140 a barrel in the summer of 2008. Real gasoline prices increased as a result, from $1.70 to more than $4 a gallon during the same period. Energy was back in the headlines.

Asia's Rise

The oil crises of the 1970s were caused by strong demand growth in the United States, Europe, and Japan combined with severe supply disruptions in the Middle East. Between 2000 and 2008, the supply side of the oil market was relatively tranquil. But demand once again outstripped supply. This demand came not from the developed world, but from emerging Asia (Killian and Hicks 2013). Figure 2.1 shows the differences between the projections of the International Energy Agency (IEA) in 2002 and those of the US Energy Information Administration (EIA) in 2003 for global oil demand for 2008 and actual demand that year. The two agencies' forecasts for global supply were quite accurate: The IEA was within 0.9 percent and the EIA within 0.1 percent of the actual figures. This is not too surprising, as most of the new production capacity slated to come online by 2008 was already in the pipeline when the reports were published.

But emerging Asia grew much faster than expected. Both the IEA and EIA forecasts assumed 5 to 6 percent annual GDP growth, as did the International Monetary Fund (IMF) and most other global economic outlooks. The region ended up posting average growth rates just under 9 percent (World Bank 2013). In China, which accounted for a large portion of the global demand surprise, economic growth became more energy intensive (Rosen and Houser 2007). As prices rose above the EIA's and IEA's $30 to $40 (in 2012 dollars) projections, so did economic growth and energy demand in oil-exporting countries newly flush with petrodollars, which pushed prices even higher (figure 2.2). The cost of crude oil for US refineries averaged $75 a barrel in 2007 and $100 a barrel in 2008 (also in 2012 dollars).

Like supply shocks, demand shocks result in seemingly outsized swings in global oil prices because oil demand and supply are both highly inelastic in the short term (Hamilton 2009b, Greene and Ahmad 2005, Goldman Sachs 2010). In the United States, transportation accounts for over 70 percent of oil consumption. Fuel substitutes in this sector are limited and Americans' ability to drive less is constrained by the availability of mass transit alternatives. Demand elasticity is even lower in developing countries. In China, rapid income growth

Figure 2.1 Difference between actual and forecasted oil demand in 2008

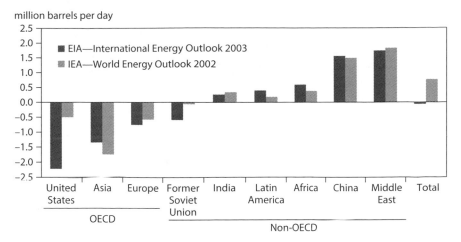

million barrels per day

EIA = Energy Information Administration; IEA = International Energy Agency; OECD = Organization for Economic Cooperation and Development

Sources: EIA (2003, 2010a); IEA (2002, 2010).

offsets some of the effects of higher oil prices and industry—still the majority of Chinese oil demand—is often able to pass price increases along to foreign consumers. In the Middle East, governments use oil export revenue to reduce the price of gasoline and diesel for domestic consumers. On the supply side, new oil production projects traditionally take years to develop and bring on-line. The only short-term buffers are consumer inventories and spare capacity in the Organization of Petroleum Exporting Countries (OPEC)—both of which were burned through rather quickly between 2002 and 2008. So when global oil demand in China and the Middle East grew faster than supply, the only way to balance the market was to destroy demand in developed countries with a higher oil price, a phenomenon known as demand rationing (Hamilton 2009b).

As in the 1970s, US natural gas prices surged alongside oil prices (figure 2.2). Wellhead natural gas prices rose from an annual average of less than $4 per thousand cubic feet in 2002 to $8.50 in 2008 (in real 2012 dollars). Because natural gas sets the price of electricity in many wholesale markets in the United States, average inflation-adjusted US power prices increased by 15 percent over the same period (EIA 2012b).

The rise in oil and gas prices increased annual US energy expenditures by roughly $700 billion in just six years (EIA 2012b).[2] That is comparable in scale to the increase in US healthcare costs over the same period (CMS 2011).

---

2. Adjusted for inflation using the GDP deflator from the Bureau of Economic Analysis (BEA), National Income Product Accounts, http://bea.gov/national/index.htm#gdp (accessed on September 8, 2013).

Figure 2.2   Oil and natural gas prices, 1864–2012

real 2012 US dollars per barrel

real 2012 US dollars per thousand cubic feet

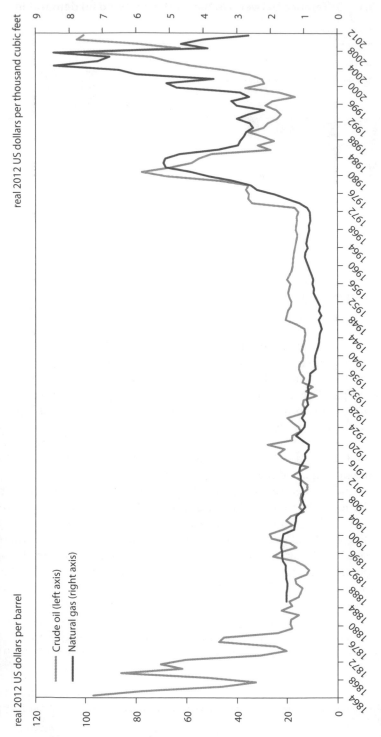

Crude oil (left axis)

Natural gas (right axis)

Note: Deflated using GDP price index.

Sources: BEA (2013); Carter et al. (2006); EIA (2013a, 2013b).

In 2008 energy expenses accounted for 10 percent of GDP, or roughly $5,000 on a per capita basis—nearly twice as high as in 2002.[3] As with the oil crises of the 1970s, this increase in energy expenses took a toll on household income and created costly dislocations in the automobile industry. Yet while the rise in real crude oil prices between 2002 and 2008 was steeper than it was during the late 1970s, the economic effect was not quite as severe. The amount of energy required to produce each unit of US economic output has declined considerably since the Carter administration thanks to a combination of technical efficiency improvements and a sectoral shift from manufacturing to service sector activity (Blanchard and Gal 2007). Also, overall inflation ran much lower between 2002 and 2008 than in the 1970s.

That said, the 2002–08 increase in oil prices still affected the US economy. Recent private sector research suggests that a sustained $10 and $20 per barrel increase in the cost of crude translates into a 0.2 and 0.5 percent reduction in GDP, respectively.[4] James Hamilton (2009a) estimates that rising oil prices between the fourth quarter of 2007 and the third quarter of 2008 cost the United States anywhere between 0.7 and 3.5 percent of GDP, depending on the methodology used to measure the effect. Hamilton argues that US economic growth would likely have been positive during that period had oil prices stayed constant. Lutz Killian notes that the same increase in global economic growth that pushed up oil prices pushed up foreign demand for US goods and services, which mitigated some of the economic damage of high oil prices. But Killian agrees that "developments in global oil and other commodity markets appear to have played an important role in the latest US recession" (Hamilton 2009a).

Supply Constraints

Until very recently, most energy analysts believed high oil and gas prices were here to stay, citing increased OPEC market share, higher royalties, political instability, and a shortage of skilled workers. At the of the end of 2007, OPEC countries possessed three-quarters of the world's proven reserves of oil (BP 2008). In theory OPEC attempts to maximize its members' long-term oil revenue through production quotas (Gately 2007, Gately et al. 2004). That requires identifying and targeting a Goldilocks global oil price—high enough to meet members' current revenue needs but low enough to avoid demand destruction or development of oil substitutes that would threaten medium- and long-term revenue prospects.[5] Oil prices reached historic highs in 2007, doubling OPEC

---

3. Energy expenditure data from EIA (2012b, table 3.5). GDP data are from the BEA's National Income Product Accounts.

4. Goldman Sachs (2011), JPMorgan (2011), Morgan Stanley (2011), Deutsche Bank (2011), Credit Suisse (2011), and Macquarie (2011).

5. In practice, there are often disagreements between OPEC members that preclude effective coordination.

export revenue, and global demand appeared to still be climbing. The IEA and other market analysts became increasingly concerned that oil producers had grown comfortable with and reliant upon high prices, and would dial back investment plans to keep them elevated (IEA 2008). The picture for natural gas did not look much better, with state-owned companies in Russia and the Middle East holding two-thirds of global proven reserves and the prospect of a natural gas OPEC looming on the horizon.[6]

Outside OPEC, higher exploration and development costs threatened to push up the long-term price of oil. According to IHS Cambridge Energy Research Associates (CERA), upstream oil and gas capital costs more than doubled between 2002 and 2008, driven by higher material prices, a shortage of skilled workers, and movement into more technically challenging oil and gas plays.[7] Political instability threatened future investment as well, with 70 percent of non-OPEC proven oil reserves in developing countries, up from 50 percent in the early 1990s (BP 2008). In addition, both OPEC and non-OPEC countries raised their tax take—the share of production revenue captured by the host government—which the IEA and others worried would further reduce investment.

As a result of these supply-side challenges, between 2002 and 2008 the IEA lowered its outlook for long-term global oil production by 11 percent and boosted its long-term oil price expectation by 250 percent. OPEC was slated to account for more than 75 percent of the modest global supply growth projected in the 2008 *World Energy Outlook*, further increasing its market power. Little growth was expected from non-OPEC producers. The natural gas story was largely the same: Between 2002 and 2008 the IEA revised its long-term global supply projection downward, by 13 percent, and expected natural gas prices to rise in line with oil.[8]

The EIA made similar adjustments to its long-term global oil and gas supply and price outlooks (EIA 2003, 2008a), as did private sector forecasters. In 2007 the National Petroleum Council, a group of leading US oil and gas companies that advise the US secretary of energy, stated that "the world is not running out of energy resources, but there are accumulating risks to continuing expansion of oil and natural gas production from the conventional sources relied upon historically. These risks create significant challenges to meeting projected energy demand" (NPC 2007). Its report included a survey of international oil company (IOC) oil and gas market outlooks. The IOC consensus at

---

6. In 2001 Iran formed the Gas Exporting Countries Forum in the hopes of eventually replicating OPEC's oil market power in natural gas. See www.gecf.org (accessed on September 8, 2013).

7. IHS CERA, Upstream Capital Costs Index (UCCI), www.ihs.com/info/cera/ihsindexes/index.aspx (accessed on September 8, 2013).

8. Oil supply projections discussed in this chapter include crude oil and natural gas liquids, unless otherwise specified, but not biofuels, condensates, and refinery processing gains.

the time was similar to the IEA's 2008 projections: stagnant non-OPEC supply, growing OPEC market share, and structurally higher prices.

Skepticism about the prospects for non-OPEC supply extended to the United States. In 2008 the IEA projected flat US oil production through 2030 (figure 2.3), keeping the United States reliant on imports for 65 percent of overall oil supply. The IEA anticipated stagnant natural gas production as well, which in the face of growing demand was projected to increase US import dependence from 14 percent to 18 percent, much of which would be supplied through new liquefied natural gas (LNG) receiving terminals along the East Coast and the Gulf of Mexico. The EIA's projections were similar (EIA 2008b), as were those from the oil and gas companies surveyed by the National Petroleum Council. The NPC (2007) found that "US oil production is generally projected to rise modestly, at best, or decline somewhat during the study time frame" and that "the concept of energy independence is not realistic in the foreseeable future." A 2006 Council on Foreign Relations task force stated that "during the next two decades, it is unlikely that the United States will be able to make a sharp reduction in its dependence on imports" and that "the real price of oil will probably continue to increase" (Deutch, Schlesinger, and Victor 2006). Even a Texas oil man turned president saw the writing on the wall and told the country in 2006 and again in 2007 that the only path to affordable energy led away from oil.

Recession and Recovery

Then, in the wake of the global financial crisis, demand among countries in the Organization for Economic Cooperation and Development (OECD) fell by 1.7 million barrels per day (bbl/d) in 2008 and by 2 million bbl/d in 2009. Oil prices collapsed. Spot prices for Brent crude—the leading international oil price benchmark—fell from a peak of $144 per barrel in early July 2008 to less than a quarter of that level in January 2009. OPEC was forced to shut down production as inventories overflowed, which helped stop the bleeding. But the real salvation for producers came from China and other emerging economies, which suffered less and recovered quicker from the crisis. Non-OECD oil demand grew by 1.4 million bbl/d per year on average during the crisis, bringing global demand and global prices back to 2007 levels by the close of 2010.

The rebound in oil prices has made economic recovery in developing countries more challenging. According to the National Bureau of Economic Research, the 2007–09 recession was the longest since the Great Depression. But the recovery has been even more atypical. US per capita GDP did not return to prerecession levels until the second quarter of 2013, four years after the recession officially ended. That makes the most recent economic recovery nearly four times longer than any in postwar US history.

Carmen Reinhart argues that the current recovery is different from others in the postwar period because of the financial crisis that preceded it. Surveying

Figure 2.3 EIA and IEA 2008 projections for oil and gas production, 1970–2030

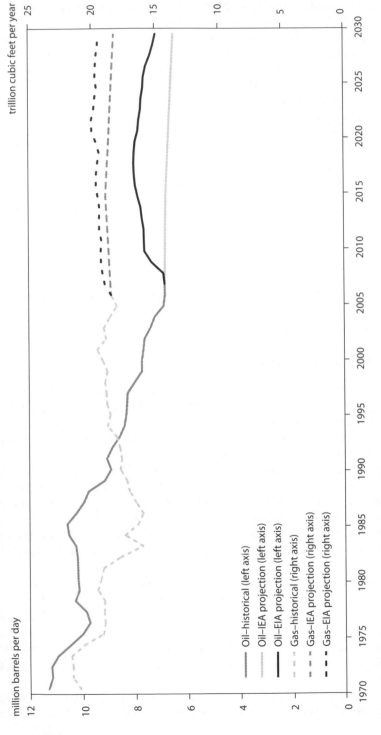

EIA = Energy Information Administration; IEA = International Energy Agency

Sources: EIA (2008b, 2012b); IEA (2008).

past business cycles around the world, she and colleague Kenneth Rogoff find that severe financial crises lead to deep recessions and long recoveries.[9] And the 2008 crisis was, of course, a whopper. Since the collapse of the housing market, high levels of household debt have limited the US consumer's ability to drive the recovery. Reinhart and Rogoff estimate that as of spring 2012, the country was only 40 percent through its deleveraging process. Making matters worse, real household incomes have fallen over the course of the recovery.

High oil prices are taking a big bite out of what little money US households have to spend, raising concerns that energy costs could threaten an already fragile economic recovery. Economists have spilled plenty of ink analyzing the relationship between oil markets and the business cycle. But almost all the focus has been on whether or not high oil prices contribute to recessions, with almost no attention paid to how oil prices shape economic recoveries. This is because, until recently, large oil price increases during recoveries were rare. As already mentioned, the price spikes preceding most US recessions—regardless of whether they contributed to the recession itself—were caused either by supply disruptions or rapid demand growth in developing countries. In those instances, by the time the country reached the trough of the recession, developed-country demand had fallen, the disruption had abated or been offset by alternative supplies, and prices had moderated. The average postwar US recovery benefited from falling crude costs, at least until the turn of the century (figure 2.4). During the past two recoveries, however, the US economy has faced oil market headwinds. A two-speed world, in which developing countries grow faster and recover quicker than developed countries, certainly has its benefits. China's resilience throughout the crisis helped keep the global economy afloat. But as most developing-country economies are more energy intensive and developing-country energy consumers less price elastic, a two-speed world also has appeared to mean structurally higher energy prices for developed-country consumers, unless global supply can keep pace.

The speed at which oil prices recovered after 2009—driven by developing-country demand, OPEC cutbacks, and a host of disruptions in supply—seemed at first to confirm the consensus among government and private sector forecasters that energy would cost much more in the future than it had in the past. In his first Oval Office address in June 2010, after the Deepwater Horizon oil spill, President Obama reiterated President Bush's call to end America's addiction to oil:

> For decades, we have known the days of cheap and easily accessible oil were numbered. For decades, we've talked and talked about the need to end America's century-long addiction to fossil fuels. And for decades, we have failed to act with the sense of urgency that this challenge requires.... As we recover from

9. Carmen M. Reinhart and Kenneth S. Rogoff, "Five Years after Crisis, No Normal Recovery," *Bloomberg*, April 2, 2012, www.bloomberg.com/news/2012-04-02/five-years-after-crisis-no-normal-recovery.html (accessed on September 8, 2013).

Figure 2.4 Change in real oil prices by months after the end of US recessions

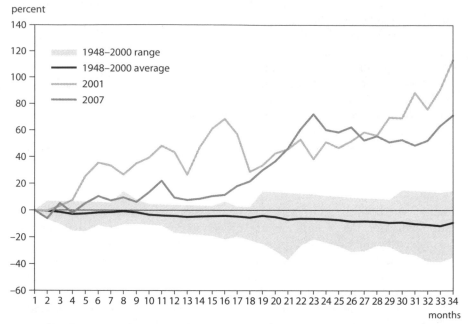

percent

Note: Crude oil price is West Texas Intermediate (WTI) spot between 1947 and 1986 and then Brent spot.

Sources: EIA (2013a); BLS (2013c); NBER (2012).

this recession, the transition to clean energy has the potential to grow our economy and create millions of jobs—but only if we accelerate that transition. Only if we seize the moment.[10]

It looked as though oil prices might help accelerate that transition by making it easier for alternative sources of energy to compete. But while President Obama was giving his speech in Washington, high prices had catalyzed a different kind of transition. Oil and gas companies were finding new ways to produce the same fossil fuels.

---

10. Office of the Press Secretary, Remarks by the President to the Nation on the BP Oil Spill, Washington, 2010, www.whitehouse.gov/the-press-office/remarks-president-nation-bp-oil-spill (accessed on September 8, 2013).

3

An Oil and Gas Renaissance

Traditionally oil and natural gas have been produced from porous and permeable underground reservoirs sealed by a separate, low-permeability rock formation. These reservoirs are filled with oil and gas produced by a source rock, usually shale, located nearby. Drilling vertically into these reservoirs, companies can extract oil and gas by taking advantage of the pressure difference between the reservoir rock and the hole that has been drilled, known as a wellbore (NPC 2011). Due to the porosity of the reservoir, oil and gas naturally migrates to the wellbore and to the surface, where it can be separated and sold. Oil and natural gas exist in different ratios in different reservoirs and are often produced together.

In 1947 the petroleum industry began injecting a cocktail of water and chemicals into low-permeability reservoirs to fracture the rock and allow trapped gas to flow to the wellbore (Montgomery and Smith 2010). These "unconventional" reservoirs can be separate from the source rock (generally referred to as "tight gas") or can be the source rock itself (as is the case with shale gas). Hydraulic fracturing can also be used to produce coal bed natural gas from coal seams (DOE 2009). In response to the energy crises of the 1970s, the federal government launched a number of programs aimed at promoting unconventional gas production. These included tax credits for gas produced from shale and other low-permeability reservoirs and research and development (R&D) focused on hydraulic fracturing (Wang and Krupnick 2013, Shellenberger et al. 2012).

It wasn't until the late 1990s, however, that these efforts bore fruit, thanks in large part to the work of one company—Mitchell Energy. Founder George Mitchell began drilling in Texas's Barnett Shale in 1981 and for more than a decade experimented with different fracturing techniques, many developed with government support. In 1997, Mitchell Energy began employing "slick water fracking," which proved more cost-effective than previous approaches. The number of new production wells drilled each year in the Barnett grew from 56 in 1996 to 518 in 2001 (Wang and Krupnick 2013). Almost all these wells were drilled vertically, but in 2002 Devon Energy acquired George Mitchell's company and began applying another innovation in the Barnett—horizontal drilling. Lower reservoir permeability means lower concentrations of natural gas. So with unconventional gas vertical drilling requires more wells to produce the same volumes than with conventional gas. And that increases costs. Horizontal drilling, which had also been a focus of the federal government's unconventional gas R&D programs, allows a company to access a greater amount of resource from a single well pad.

The combination of hydraulic fracturing and horizontal drilling made shale production commercially viable. All that was needed to scale it up was capital. And when gas prices began climbing at the turn of the century, capital began to flow. The number of natural gas rigs operating in the United States doubled between 2002 and 2007, driven by shale gas's increasingly attractive economics (figure 3.1), and the average number of exploration wells drilled each month rose from 70 to 230. Natural gas production grew by 25 percent between 2007 and 2012 as newly discovered resources were developed (EIA 2013b). The Potential Gas Committee's estimate of technically recoverable natural gas resources in the United States more than doubled in less than a decade and shale has pushed proven natural gas reserves to historically high levels (figure 3.2).[1]

Natural gas prices collapsed during the financial crisis just as oil did. But because of the surge in supply, gas prices continued to decline while oil prices recovered (figure 3.3). Unlike oil, which is a globally traded commodity, natural gas trade is largely confined to North America. The United States has long imported significant quantities of natural gas from Canada and Mexico through an integrated North American pipeline network, but only minor amounts of liquefied natural gas (LNG) from the rest of the world—less than 4 percent of total supply at the peak. As a relatively isolated market, North America has what is known as gas-on-gas pricing. The price of gas is determined by North American supply and demand for gas, with a futures market based off the Henry Hub distribution center in Louisiana. In contrast, Europe, Korea, and Japan rely on foreign gas, much of it delivered as LNG, that is generally linked to the international price of crude. A 25 percent increase in US production is only a 4 percent increase in total global supply, which in an integrated market would have only a modest effect on price. But within the North American market, a 25 percent increase in US output was enough to cut natural gas prices by two-thirds.

---

1. Potential Gas Committee, "Potential Gas Committee Reports Significant Increase in Magnitude of US Natural Gas Resource Base," press release, April 9, 2013, http://potentialgas.org/press-release (accessed on September 8, 2013).

Figure 3.1   Natural gas prices and drilling activity, 1996–2012

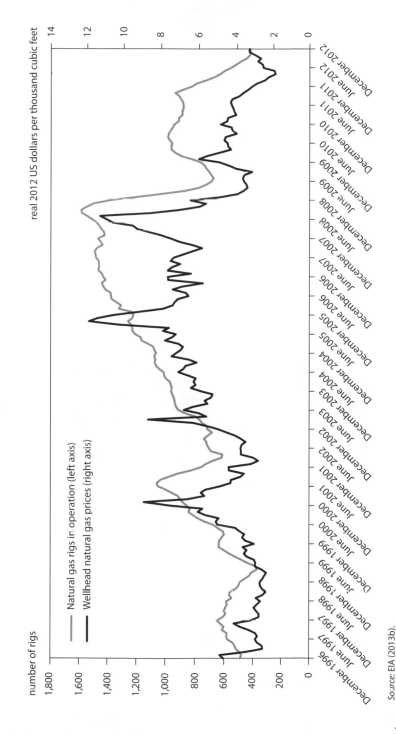

Source: EIA (2013b).

Figure 3.2   Proven natural gas reserves, 1950–2011

trillion cubic feet

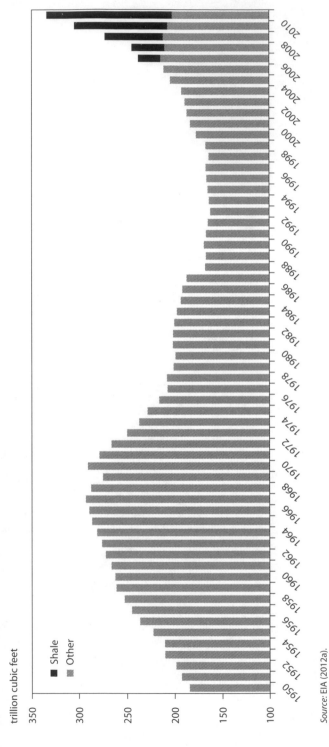

■ Shale
■ Other

Source: EIA (2012a).

Figure 3.3   Crude and natural gas prices, 1996–2012

2012 US dollars per million British thermal units

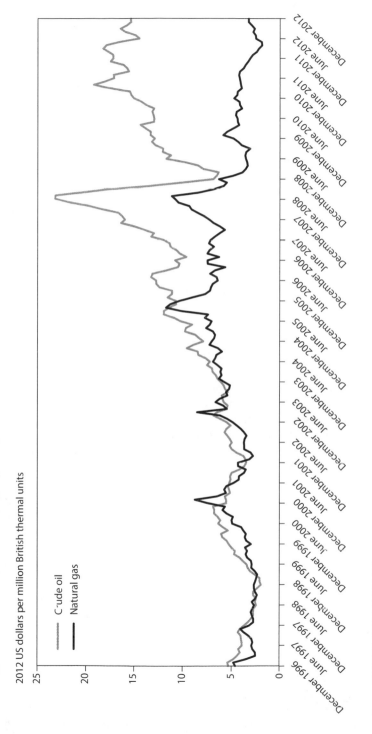

Sources: EIA (2013b, 2013g); BLS (2013c).

Broadening to Oil

The fall in US natural gas prices has opened an unprecedented gap between the cost of oil and the cost of gas. When measured on the same basis—2012 dollars per million British thermal units—oil and gas have traditionally cost about the same (figure 3.3). This was true as recently as the end of 2008. Yet in 2012, oil cost more than six times as much as natural gas. This catalyzed the second stage of the US fossil fuel turnaround. As the relative profitability of oil production improved, that's where the industry focused its attention.

The combination of horizontal drilling and hydraulic fracturing has come to dominate domestic exploration. In 2002 there were 50 to 100 horizontal drilling rigs operating in the United States. In 2012 there were 1,100 to 1,200. The combination of techniques can be used to produce oil as well as gas. In 2008 there were four times more rigs drilling for gas than for oil. By 2012 that ratio had switched (figure 3.4), with the Bakken Formation in North Dakota and parts of Montana and Saskatchewan accounting for much of the rise in oil-focused drilling activity. North Dakota has long been an oil-producing state, but a minor one. Between 1980 and 2000, the state produced 100,000 barrels per day (bbl/d) on average and held 150 million to 300 million barrels of proven reserves, 1 to 2 percent of the US total in both cases (EIA 2013g). The US Geological Survey (USGS) estimated there were only 151 million barrels of undiscovered but technically recoverable oil in the Bakken Formation, enough for only a few years of additional production.[2] As companies began applying in North Dakota what they had learned from shale gas drilling, the picture changed dramatically. By 2008 proven reserves had doubled, prompting the USGS to conduct a new resource assessment. This one found 3,645 million barrels—10 percent of the US total. By 2010 proven reserves had grown to 1,814 million barrels and by the end of 2012, North Dakota was producing 770,000 barrels of oil per day. In 2013 the USGS doubled its estimates of the Bakken's technically recoverable reserves.[3]

Tight oil, as the new Bakken output is called, is being produced in other parts of the country as well. Production in the Eagle Ford, Spraberry, and other plays in Texas and New Mexico added roughly 1 million barrels per day to total US oil output between 2008 and 2012. Production is ramping up in Wyoming, Colorado, Oklahoma, and Kansas. Promising basins are being explored in the East, such as the Utica Shale under Ohio and Pennsylvania. There is further exploration of the massive Monterey Formation in southern California. Thanks primarily to this surge in tight oil production, US crude

---

2. US Department of the Interior, "Bakken Formation Oil Assessment in North Dakota, Montana Will Be Updated by U.S. Geological Survey," press release, May 19, 2011, www.doi.gov/news/press-releases/Bakken-Formation-Oil-Assessment-in-North-Dakota-Montana-will-be-updated-by-US-Geological-Survey.cfm (accessed on September 8, 2013).

3. US Geological Survey, "USGS Releases New Oil and Gas Assessment for Bakken and Three Forks Formations," press release, April 30, 2013, www.doi.gov/news/pressreleases/usgs-releases-new-oil-and-gas-assessment-for-bakken-and-three-forks-formations.cfm (accessed on September 8, 2013).

Figure 3.4   Number of rigs drilling primarily for oil versus natural gas, 1999–2013

number of rigs

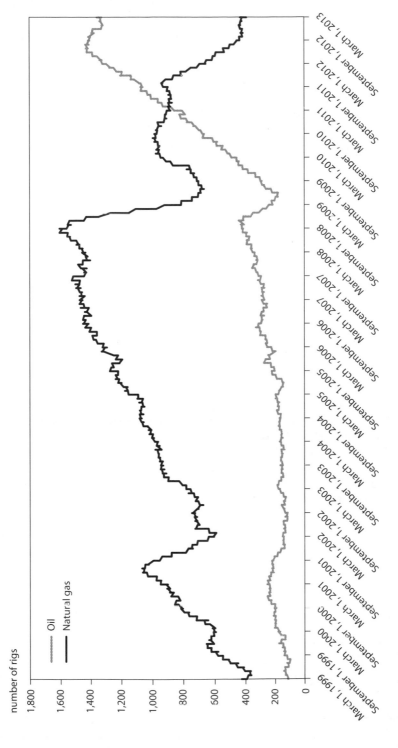

Source: Baker Hughes (2012).

output has reversed its decades-long decline, growing by 1.5 million barrels per day between 2008 and 2012 (figure 3.5).

Shale gas production has helped increase the US oil supply in other ways as well. Along with the dry natural gas piped into homes and used to run power plants, shale, like other gas wells, produces what are called natural gas liquids (NGLs). These liquids can be used instead of naphtha, a crude oil derivative, in chemical production, and are thus classified as oil by the Energy Information Administration (EIA), International Energy Agency (IEA), and other statistical agencies. Most US petrochemical companies use NGLs instead of naphtha as their primary feedstock. Shale gas production—along with tight oil production, which also produces NGLs—has increased the country's NGL supply by 600,000 bbl/d, bringing the growth in total US oil supply between 2008 and 2012 to 2.1 million bbl/d.

The recent reallocation of drilling rigs from shale gas to tight oil plays has not reduced US natural gas supply growth as much as one might think. Tight oil reservoirs generally contain associated natural gas as well, which is produced alongside the oil. Given the recent drop in gas prices, many gas-rich plays are no longer economic. But as associated gas is a secondary factor in the economics of tight oil plays, it keeps flowing even when gas prices are low.[4]

The Bakken and other tight oil plays are not the only places where US crude output is growing. Companies are employing enhanced oil recovery techniques to increase the amount of oil produced from conventional fields, including carbon dioxide (CO_2) injection, which displaces oil from a well and increases production. This carries environmental as well as energy supply benefits, as the CO_2 is sequestered rather than released into the atmosphere, thus lowering greenhouse gas concentrations. Processes such as this, which improve a reservoir's or a well's estimated ultimate recovery, have been instrumental in oil and gas reserve growth in the past.

The economics of deepwater drilling are also more favorable than a decade ago, thanks to technological advances as well as high oil prices. Offshore production in the Gulf of Mexico doubled between 1990 and 2009. While the Deepwater Horizon disaster and subsequent drilling moratorium dealt a blow to Gulf production, exploration work has started to recover and some large new fields have been discovered. Since sea ice levels have dropped due to climate change, the Alaskan Arctic is also being explored as a potential site of oil and gas production. Even potential oil shale plays, such as the Green River Formation in Colorado, Utah, and Wyoming, are getting a closer look.

America's Oil and Gas Future

Whether the recent surge in US oil and gas production is the beginning of a structural expansion in US supply, as in the early 1900s, or just a momentary respite from a structural decline, as in the late 1970s and early 1980s, remains to

---

4. Industry productivity has also improved, allowing companies to produce more from fewer wells.

Figure 3.5 US oil production, 1973–2012

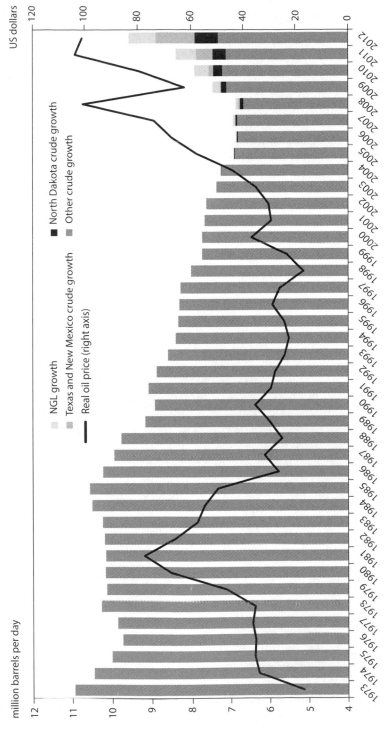

million barrels per day

US dollars

Legend:
- NGL growth
- Texas and New Mexico crude growth
- Real oil price (right axis)
- North Dakota crude growth
- Other crude growth

Note: Oil includes crude oil and natural gas liquids (NGL).

Source: EIA (2013a).

23

be seen. The industry is still in the early stages of understanding and exploring newly discovered shale gas and tight oil resources and newly accessible fields in the Arctic and deep in the Gulf of Mexico. Much will depend on what happens to the price of oil, which depends on how producers in other parts of the world respond to the prospect of increased US supply (see chapter 4). Human capital and infrastructure constraints could limit future production potential. Policy also will play a major role in shaping future US oil and gas supply. There are active and passionate debates under way about how aggressively to develop oil and gas resources on federal lands and the best way to regulate frontier oil and gas production, whether through hydrofracking or deepwater development.

Given the uncertainty surrounding the size of the resource, the oil and gas price outlook, and the future policy environment, forecasts of future US supply growth vary widely. The EIA has significantly revised its oil and gas projections in recent years. In 2006 the EIA projected 6.4 million bbl/d of crude oil and NGL production in 2030. Its 2013 projection is 9.2 million bbl/d (figure 3.6). For natural gas, the EIA's 2013 projection for US production in 2030 is 81.6 billion cubic feet per day (Bcfd), up from 53.2 Bcfd in the 2006 forecast (figure 3.7). In its 2013 *Annual Energy Outlook* report, the EIA included a side case that analyzed the effect of higher than expected unconventional oil and gas resources. In this scenario production grows to 14.6 million bbl/d and 101.1 Bcfd of oil and gas, respectively, by 2030. At the time of publication, US oil and gas production appeared to be following this trajectory.[5]

The IEA's 2012 outlook projects US oil production will grow to 11.1 million bbl/d by 2020, a 35 percent upward revision from its 2011 projections and a little higher than the EIA's 2013 reference case scenario (figures 3.8 and 3.9). In both the IEA and EIA outlooks, US oil production peaks by 2020 as the most promising tight oil plays are exhausted. As tight oil wells generally decline faster than conventional wells, US oil production falls to 9.2 million bbl/d by 2035 in both forecasts. On gas, the IEA is a little more conservative than the EIA, projecting 77.5 Bcfd of production by 2035.

A number of private sector forecasts are similar to the EIA's 2013 reference case scenario. ExxonMobil projects that US crude oil and NGL supply will reach 9.8 million bbl/d by 2020, after which, in its outlook, the supply modestly declines (table 3.1, figure 3.8, and figure 3.9). Natural gas production peaks at 74 Bcfd in 2030, very close to the EIA estimates (ExxonMobil 2013).[6] BP sees crude oil and NGL production reaching 11.5 million bbl/d and natural gas production reaching 89.4 Bcfd by 2030, a little higher than the EIA forecasts (BP 2013).

---

5. Adam Sieminski, "Outlook for shale gas and tight oil development in the U.S.," presentation at the Bank of America/Merrill Lynch Global Emerging Markets Spring Investor Conference, April 20, 2013, Washington, www.eia.gov/pressroom/presentations/sieminski_04202013.pdf (accessed on September 8, 2013).

6. ExxonMobil has released a 2013 outlook with a more optimistic global production forecast but has not published US-specific production estimates.

Figure 3.6   EIA projections of US oil production, 1973–2035

million barrels per day

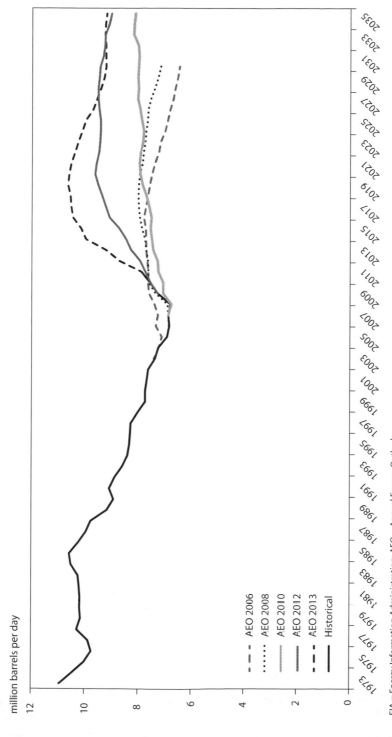

AEO 2006
AEO 2008
AEO 2010
AEO 2012
AEO 2013
Historical

EIA = Energy Information Administration; AEO = Annual Energy Outlook

Sources: EIA (2006, 2008b, 2010b, 2012b, 2012c, 2013e).

Figure 3.7 EIA projections of US natural gas production, 1973–2035

billion cubic feet per year

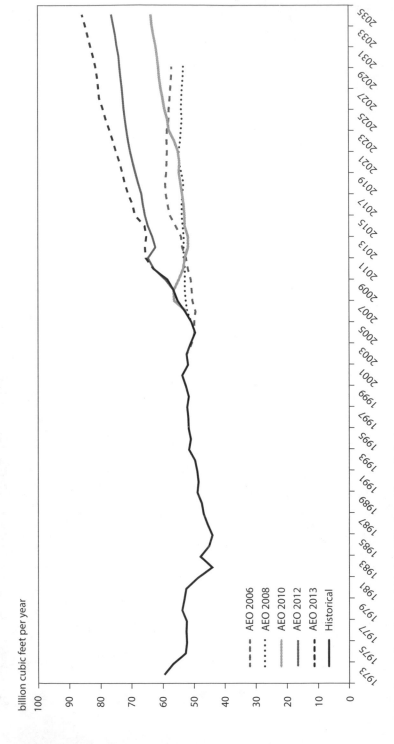

EIA = Energy Information Administration; AEO = Annual Energy Outlook

Sources: EIA (2006, 2008b, 2010b, 2012b, 2012c, 2013e).

Table 3.1 Comparing US supply projections

Organization	Publication	Year	Scenario	Oil production[a] (million barrels per day)			Natural gas production (billion cubic feet per day)		
				2020	2030	2035	2020	2030	2035
Energy Information Administration (EIA)	Annual Energy Outlook	2013	Reference	10.6	9.2	9.2	72.9	81.6	85.9
		2008	Reference	7.9	7.2	n.a.	53.7	53.2	n.a.
International Energy Agency (IEA)	World Energy Outlook	2012	New policies	11.1	10.2	9.2	72.1	75.9	77.5
		2008	Current policies	6.7	6.5	n.a.	51.0	49.9	n.a.
National Petroleum Council (NPC)	Prudent Development	2011	Limited	n.a.	n.a.	5.6	n.a.	n.a.	53.7
			High potential	n.a.	n.a.	14.6	n.a.	n.a.	88.4
Wood Mackenzie	American Petroleum Institute (API) Study	2011	Current path	8.8	9.0	n.a.	67.3	74.5	n.a.
			Development policy	10.7	15.4	n.a.	75.0	96.9	n.a.
Citigroup	Energy 2020	2012		14.1	n.a.	n.a.	76.0	n.a.	n.a.
IHS CERA (Cambridge Energy Research Associates)	America's New Energy Future	2012		12.2	11.3	12.0	81.9	92.9	100.5
ExxonMobil	Outlook for Energy	2012		9.8	9.3	8.5	71.1	74.0	71.1
BP	Energy Outlook 2030	2013		11.5	11.4	n.a.	80.2	89.4	n.a.
Authors' scenarios			Pre-shale	8.2	7.8	6.9	58.3	60.8	57.8
			Conservative	9.6	9.4	9.0	68.6	73.8	76.5
			Optimistic	13.0	14.5	14.1	82.4	94.0	97.9

n.a. = not available

a. Includes crude oil and natural gas liquids.

Source: Authors' calculations.

Figure 3.8 Government and private sector US oil production projections, 1973–2035

million barrels per day

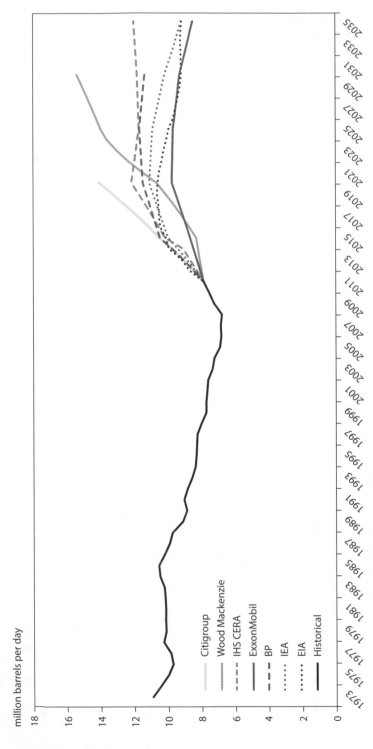

IEA = International Energy Agency; EIA = Energy Information Administration

Note: Includes crude oil and natural gas liquids.

Sources: EIA (2013e); IEA (2012a); Morse et al. (2012); ExxonMobil (2013); BP (2013); Wood Mackenzie (2011); IHS CERA (2012); National Petroleum Council (NPC 2011).

Figure 3.9   Government and private sector US natural gas production projections, 1973–2035

billion cubic feet per year

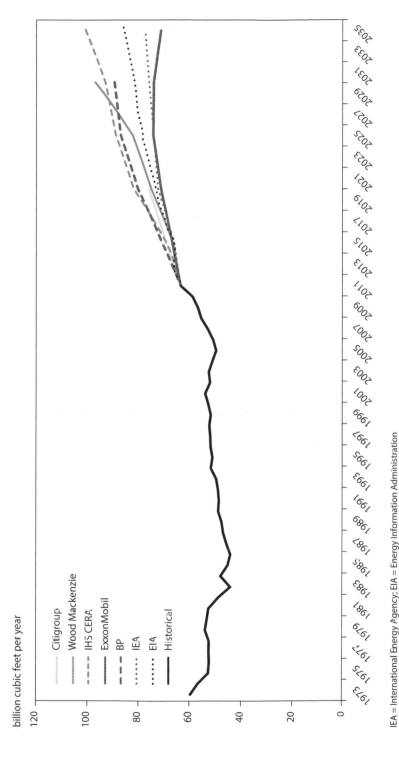

IEA = International Energy Agency; EIA = Energy Information Administration

Sources: EIA (2013e); IEA (2012a); Morse et al. (2012); ExxonMobil (2013); BP (2013); Wood Mackenzie (2011); IHS CERA (2012); National Petroleum Council (NPC 2011).

Other private sector estimates, however, are considerably more bullish and closer to the EIA's high oil and gas resource side case. On the liquids side, Citigroup estimates that US crude and NGL production could reach 14.1 million bbl/d by 2020, an astounding 80 percent increase in total US output in less than a decade (Morse et al. 2012). Consultancy Wood Mackenzie (2011) sees slower growth over the next few years but believes US crude and NGL production could reach 15.4 million bbl/d by 2030. IHS Cambridge Energy Research Associates (IHS CERA 2012) expects roughly 12 million bbl/d of output between 2020 and 2035. The 2011 report of the National Petroleum Council (NPC 2011) describes a high potential scenario in which 14.6 million bbl/d of crude oil and NGL production is possible by 2035. On the natural gas side, Citigroup projects US production will increase to 81.9 Bcfd by 2020. Wood Mackenzie expects production to reach 75 Bcfd in 2020 and 97 Bcfd in 2030. IHS CERA has the most aggressive private forecast, with US production rising to 82 Bcfd in 2020 and 100.5 Bcfd by 2035.

Several caveats should be kept in mind when comparing the above forecasts. First, the IEA, EIA, ExxonMobil, BP, and IHS CERA projections are integrated supply-demand assessments, meaning they dynamically model the effect of increased energy supply on energy prices and the effect of changes in energy prices on energy demand. The NPC, Citigroup, and Wood Mackenzie assessments do not. Second, the forecasts are not all looking at the same future. The EIA projections assume no new policy beyond what was adopted at the beginning of 2013. The IEA projections assume that currently proposed policy is adopted and the ExxonMobil, BP, and IHS CERA projections incorporate policies each organization views as most likely to be adopted in the future.

The Wood Mackenzie, NPC, and Citigroup estimates, on the other hand, are upper-bound projections of what is possible given the nature of the resource and the economics of production, not necessarily these organizations' views of what is most likely to occur. Wood Mackenzie assumes that areas currently closed to development—the Eastern Gulf of Mexico, federal lands in the Rocky Mountains, offshore fields along the West and East Coasts, the Alaska National Wildlife Refuge, the Alaskan National Petroleum Reserve, the Alaskan offshore, and the portion of the Marcellus Shale in New York state— are opened and that both federal and state governments work to expedite drilling permits and make environmental regulation more industry-friendly. Wood Mackenzie then compares this future with a scenario in which no new areas are opened for exploration, Gulf of Mexico drilling permitting continues to be slow, and hypothetical federal hydrofracking regulations slow the rate of shale gas and tight oil development. The NPC (2011) describes its high-potential scenario as one of "substantial advances in technology, and regulatory burdens that are not significantly different than today" and compares that with a limited-potential scenario, described as "limited resource access, constrained technology development, as well as greater regulatory barriers." The Citigroup report "focuses on the possible rather than providing a forecast of what's to come" (Morse et al. 2012).

Policy explains some of the variations in recent forecasts, but differences in assumptions about the size and cost of US oil and gas resources also play a major role. IHS CERA has the most optimistic estimates for future US gas production, but does not assume any significant increase in access to federal lands relative to current levels going forward. Citigroup believes a threefold (2.5 million bbl/d) increase in Gulf of Mexico oil production is possible by 2020 in areas currently open for development, while Wood Mackenzie forecasts a 1.2 million bbl/d increase despite opening up the eastern Gulf of Mexico. IHS CERA expects deepwater production to grow by only a couple hundred thousand barrels per day between now and 2020 and then fall by roughly half between 2020 and 2035.

There is an emerging consensus that the current oil and gas boom has at least another decade to run, and with each forecast revision, the gap between projections narrows. But the magnitude of the uncertainty surrounding future US supply is still very large and must be kept in mind when assessing the boom's economic effects. Unconventional gas development has a bit of a lead on unconventional oil, so there is more agreement on future US production. The standard deviation of the natural gas production forecasts listed in table 3.1 is 5.4 and 11 percent of the mean for 2020 and 2030, respectively, compared with 12.3 and 20.8 percent for oil. Yet in absolute terms, the remaining uncertainty about future US gas production is still sizeable—a 23 Bcfd delta between the lower- and upper-end estimates for production in 2030. That is more than the total current natural gas consumption in China and Japan combined, and three-quarters of the size of global LNG trade today. The variation in projected oil production is even bigger. The difference between the upper-bound and lower-bound forecasts for 2030 listed in table 3.1 is as large as total US oil production in 2008. At 15.4 million bbl/d of output, the upper-end estimate, the United States would easily surpass Saudi Arabia and Russia to become the world's largest oil producer. And the 6 million bbl/d delta between current projections is itself larger than any oil producer in the world other than Saudi Arabia and Russia.

US Energy Independence?

Encouraged by the more optimistic supply forecasts discussed above, some commentators have begun to predict a development that politicians have long talked about but that the analytical community has largely dismissed: US energy independence. *Energy independence* is a loaded term, meaning different things to different people and implying potential economic and geopolitical benefits that may be elusive in practice. We start by assessing what recent supply and demand projections mean for net US energy imports, the most basic and common metric used to assess energy independence. Chapter 4 discusses what economic benefits this change in US energy trade might bring, and in what ways the United States will remain vulnerable to supply disruptions in global energy markets. Analysis of the geopolitical implications, a critical and complex question, is outside the scope of this book.

Both government and private sector forecasts expect the US energy trade deficit to fall in the years ahead, and many expect it to fall substantially. Supply affects price and price affects demand, so integrated modeling is required for a robust projection of the US energy trade balance. Taking this approach, the EIA revised its projection of US dependence on imported energy in 2030 downward from 33 percent in the 2006 outlook and to 11 percent in 2013 edition (figure 3.10). The IEA projects a 4 percent energy trade deficit that year. In BP's outlook, US dependence on imported energy falls to 1 percent by 2030. ExxonMobil expects higher natural gas imports in the future than the EIA, IEA, or BP, so overall energy import dependency only falls to 16 percent (figure 3.11).

The Citigroup analyses focus on oil and gas supply and gasoline and diesel demand. The projections in figure 3.11 assess the effect of these estimates when combined with the EIA's supply and demand projections for other energy sources. This is an imprecise approach, as changing oil and gas supply changes overall energy demand and supply from other energy sources, but it is a reasonable upper-bound estimate of the effect on overall energy import dependence. Using the Citigroup projections, the United States becomes a net energy exporter by 2020. Citigroup is not alone in predicting that the United States will become energy independent in roughly a decade (Verleger 2012, Adkins and Molchanov 2012). Combined with EIA demand and non-oil-and-gas-supply projections, Wood Mackenzie's oil and gas production forecasts suggest that the United States could reduce its net energy imports to zero by 2027. Under IHS CERA's more conservative oil production forecasts and more ambitious natural gas demand estimates, however, US net energy imports fall to about 10 percent of production but stay at roughly that level through 2035.

Assessing America's Oil and Gas Future

We are loath to predict future US oil and gas supply, given how dramatically both public and private sector projections have shifted in just a couple years, and in any event are poorly suited to do so given our backgrounds and expertise. Instead, in the coming chapters we analyze the economic, environmental, and trade effects of two production scenarios that capture the range of forecasts discussed above. For this analysis, we use the National Energy Modeling System (NEMS), the model the EIA uses to produce its *Annual Energy Outlook*, which allows for an apples-to-apples comparison between our results and current EIA projections. Also, NEMS is publicly available and extensively documented, which enables others to reproduce our results. A full description of the model and the assumptions used in this analysis is available in appendix A.

As our goal is to evaluate what recent changes in US oil and gas production trends mean for economic growth, environmental quality, and international trade policy, we start by establishing a baseline against which to measure current projections—that is, what the oil and gas supply future looked like before the shale gas and tight oil boom. To do this, we reduced NEMS estimates of technically recoverable resources (TRR) to levels the EIA used for its 2008 projections. We also limited offshore drilling to areas that were open for de-

Figure 3.10   EIA projections of future US dependence on imported energy, 1973–2035

percent share of total consumption

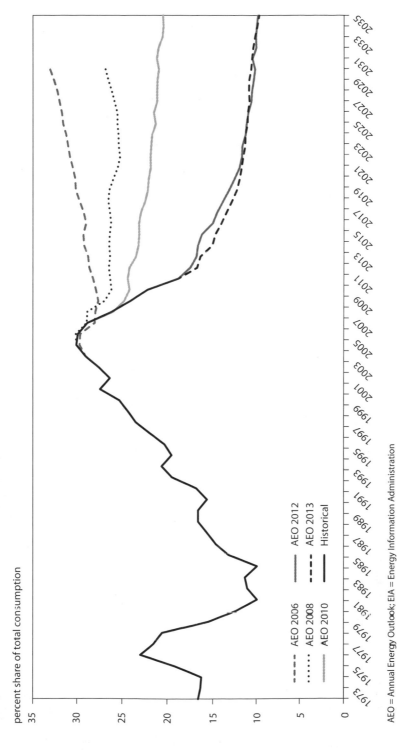

AEO = Annual Energy Outlook; EIA = Energy Information Administration

Sources: EIA (2006, 2008b, 2010b, 2012b, 2012c, 2013e).

Figure 3.11 Government and private sector projections of future US dependence on imported energy, 1973–2035

percent share of total consumption

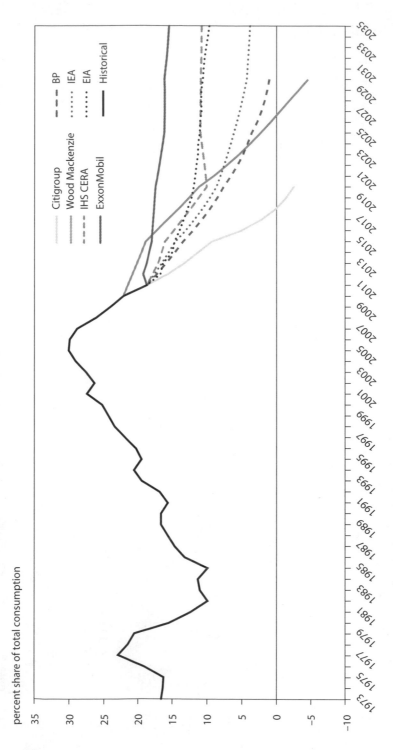

IEA = International Energy Agency; EIA = Energy Information Administration

Sources: EIA (2013e); IEA (2012a); Morse et al. (2012); ExxonMobil (2013a); BP (2013); Wood Mackenzie (2011); IHS CERA (2012); National Petroleum Council (NPC 2011).

velopment in 2008, specifically the western and central Gulf of Mexico. In this pre-shale case, US oil[7] production peaks at 8.2 million bbl/d in 2020 and then declines to 6.9 million bbl/d by 2035 (table 3.1). This is a little higher than the EIA's 2008 projections, due mostly to higher projected oil prices creating incentives for more production, even with the same resource base. Natural gas production stays roughly flat at 2011 levels throughout the projection period.

We then model two post-shale production futures. Our conservative scenario is consistent with the more restrained production forecasts above, such as the EIA's 2013 low oil and gas resources side case, ExxonMobil's 2012 projections, and, for natural gas, the IEA's 2012 numbers. Under this scenario, oil production grows to 9.6 million bbl/d by 2020 and then declines modestly to 9 million bbl/d by 2035. Gas production grows to 68.6 Bcfd in 2020 and 76.5 Bcfd in 2035.

Our optimistic scenario is consistent with the more ambitious projections from Wood Mackenzie, Citigroup, IHS CERA, and the EIA's 2013 high oil and gas resources case. In modeling this scenario, we use a number of assumptions from the EIA 2012 high TRR case—the closest EIA scenario available at the time we began our modeling—including closer spacing for tight oil and shale gas wells, a 50 percent increase in estimated ultimate recovery relative to the EIA reference case, and a more than twofold increase in estimated unproved tight oil and shale gas resources. In addition, we open all areas of the outer continental shelf (OCS) in the lower 48 states to offshore drilling, double the unproven resource estimates for these areas, and reduce drilling delays. In Alaska we triple OCS resource estimates and allow for Arctic exploration. Under these assumptions, US oil production grows to 13 million bbl/d in 2020 and plateaus at 14 million to 14.5 million bbl/d between 2030 and 2035. Natural gas production grows to 82.4 Bcfd in 2020 and 97.9 Bcfd in 2035.

By comparing our conservative and optimistic scenarios to a scenario with pre-shale policy, technology, and resource assumptions, we can evaluate the economic, environmental, and trade effects of the US oil and natural gas boom specifically, holding other variables, such as macroeconomic changes unrelated to oil and gas production, constant. The differences among the pre-shale, conservative, and optimistic scenarios reflect a combination of policy, technology, and resource factors—not the potential outcomes of any discrete decision facing policymakers today. The resource base could prove as abundant as reflected in our high scenario, but future production could fall short due to regulatory barriers to development. Likewise, production could disappoint despite policy support if more conservative estimates of resource cost and availability prove correct. Our objective here is to put the overall changes in the oil and gas supply outlook over the past four or five years in an economic context to help policymakers understand what it means for future US employment and economic output, appreciate the distributional consequences, and evaluate and manage trade and environmental policy implications.

---

7. Includes crude oil and NGLs but excludes biofuels, condensates, and refinery gains.

4

Economic Impact

Energy, along with labor, land, and capital, is a basic ingredient in America's economic growth formula. Yet energy has traditionally been left out of macroeconomic analysis (Aghion and Howitt 2009). Early economic models, such as the Solow growth model and the underlying Cobb-Douglas production function, focused on capital and labor as the two factors of production. In those models, more people and more labor mean more growth. But the increase in economic output from each additional worker or dollar of capital investment diminishes over time, unless technological change allows the economy to use labor and capital more efficiently. This technological change, called multifactor productivity or total factor productivity in economics, is crucial for long-term economic growth. Over time, economists incorporated energy and other natural resources as additional factors of production in growth models, demonstrating the importance of the energy sector in economic performance (Stern 2011). Increased supply of affordable energy and improved energy efficiency can boost potential economic growth. And energy often can substitute for other factors of production, making an economy more resilient to changes in factor costs.

Growth in energy supply has played an important role in the United States' past economic success. The development of coal reserves in the 19th century led to a tenfold increase in total US energy production between 1850 and 1920, making the Industrial Revolution possible (Schurr and Netschert 1960; EIA 2012b, 2013d). Following World War II, energy supply doubled in just 25 years, helping to facilitate postwar economic expansion. Between 1970 and the current oil and gas boom, domestic fossil fuel production was relatively flat, with nuclear and imported energy making up for the shortfall in domestic fossil fuel supply.

Efficiency has played a major role in ensuring supply sufficiency as well. Between 1850 and 1900 the amount of energy required for each unit of economic output fell by half, thanks to efficient wood stoves and fuel switching from wood to coal, from which more energy could be captured (Schurr and Netschert 1960, EIA 2012b, BEA 2013, Carter et al. 2006). The energy intensity of the US economy increased during the industrial boom of the early 1900s, but by 1930 had resumed its structural decline. When domestic energy supply growth stagnated in the 1970s, efficiency became even more important. In 2012 the US economy required less than half as much energy for each unit of economic output as in 1972.

Changes in energy prices also affect economic growth (Ayres and Warr 2005). Lower energy prices mean lower production costs for businesses, lower prices on goods and services, and lower household energy bills, all of which allow for greater consumption. Higher energy prices reduce real household income and increase business production costs. If they are sustained, they feed through into headline inflation, which can prompt central bankers to raise interest rates. The average price Americans pay for energy has risen considerably over the past century, thanks primarily to growing dependence on increasingly expensive oil and, to a lesser extent, natural gas. That has kept primary energy expenditures at 3 to 4 percent of GDP on average, despite significant energy-intensity improvements (Schurr and Netschert 1960, EIA 2012b, BEA 2013, Carter et al. 2006). The price of oil has proved far more volatile than that of coal or wood, with primary energy expenditures as a share of GDP spiking to 8 percent following the supply shocks of the late 1920s and 6 percent following the 2000–08 demand shock. The price of delivered energy is considerably higher than that of primary energy because it includes the cost of transportation, refining crude oil into petroleum products, and converting coal, natural gas, and other fuels into electricity. Delivered energy expenditures peaked at 13.7 percent of GDP in 1981 before falling to 7 percent of GDP by the mid-1990s (Houser 2013). Between 2002 and 2008, delivered energy expenditures rose again, from 6.2 percent of GDP to 9.9 percent of GDP. Expenditures dropped to 7.6 percent of GDP during the financial crisis and then rebounded to 9.1 percent of GDP in 2011. As discussed in chapter 2, these price spikes inflict economic damage beyond direct losses in business and consumer purchasing power.

Finally, energy plays an important role in shaping the United States' international economic position. On net, the United States spent $284 billion on imported energy in 2012, with oil accounting for the overwhelming majority. While down from a peak of $408 billion in 2008, this still accounts for 1.8 percent of GDP, on par with the US bilateral trade deficit with China (figure 4.1). And unlike trade with China, the sharp increase in the energy trade deficit since 2000 is more due to an increase in price than quantity, which erodes US terms of trade and overall economic growth.

Given the economic costs of high oil and gas prices in recent years (chapter 2), there is considerable excitement surrounding the potential economic bene-

Figure 4.1 US trade deficit in energy and with China as a share of GDP, 1962–2012

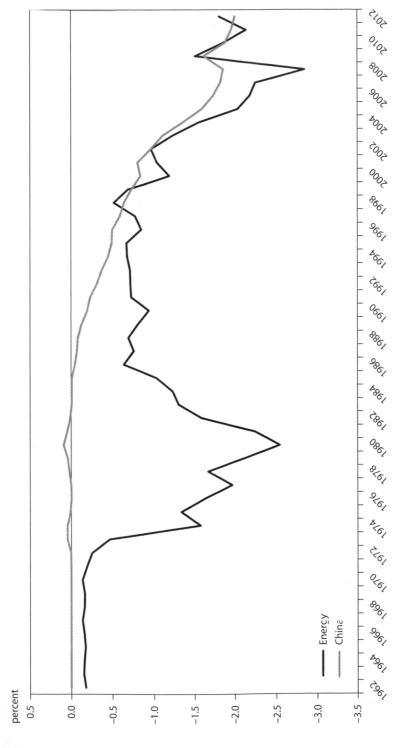

percent

Source: UN Statistics Division, Commodity Trade Statistics Database, 2012.

fits of the current boom in US oil and gas supply.[1] The drilling activity taking place from North Dakota to Pennsylvania is boosting economic output and employment in those areas and beyond by creating demand for a wide range of goods and services. Higher production has lowered domestic natural gas and electricity prices already and could do the same for the price of oil. That means household incomes will go farther and business expenses will be lower. A significant decline in net oil import expenditures could improve US terms of trade and make the economy as a whole better off.

Existing Analysis

Both government and private sector forecasters have assessed the effects of rising US oil and gas supply on the future of US energy, but analysis of its economic implications has struggled to keep pace. A 2011 Wood Mackenzie study (from which the Wood Mackenzie supply projections in chapter 3 are taken) finds that pro-oil-and-gas-development policies that included increased access to federal lands currently closed to production offshore, onshore, and in the Alaska National Wildlife Refuge could create 1.4 million jobs by 2030 (Wood Mackenzie 2011). The American Chemistry Council (ACC 2011) claims that increased chemical industry investment due to a shale-driven reduction in US natural gas prices could create over 400,000 jobs and $132 billion in economic activity. McKinsey & Co. estimates that increased unconventional oil and gas production and associated infrastructure investment and manufacturing competitiveness could add between $380 billion and $690 billion in annual economic output and 1 million to 1.7 million jobs in 2020 (Lund et al. 2013). And consulting firm IHS Cambridge Energy Research Associates (CERA) estimates that the unconventional oil and gas boom will deliver 3.5 million jobs and $475 billion in annual economic output by 2035 (IHS CERA 2012; see chapter 3 supply projections).

All four studies use input-output (I-O) models to examine the effects of increased gas, oil supply, and associated infrastructure and manufacturing investment on employment and the economy. By mapping the relation between industries and the flow of goods and services through the economy, I-O models are used to assess the effect of an increase in output from one industry on both employment in that industry and output and employment in other industries. For example, if we want to understand the economic effects of a $1 million increase in oil and gas production, an I-O model can be used to estimate how many jobs in the oil and gas industry such an increase in production would support. In economic parlance, this is called a direct effect. But an increase in oil and gas production creates demand for intermediate goods and

---

1. David Ignatius, "An Economic Boom Ahead?" *Washington Post*, May 4, 2012, www.washington-post.com/opinions/an-economic-boom-ahead/2012/05/04/gIQAbj5K2T_story.html (accessed on September 8, 2013; "America's Red State Growth Corridors," *Wall Street Journal*, February 25, 2013.

services, such as steel, trucking, lawyers, and engineers. This is called an indirect effect, which can also be assessed using an I-O model. Further, when oil and gas employees, or employees of industries supporting oil and gas, spend their paychecks—think restaurants, real estate, and arts and entertainment—more economic activity and employment are created. This is known as an induced effect. The Wood Mackenzie, ACC, McKinsey and IHS CERA studies count direct, indirect, and induced effects in their jobs and economic output estimates.

The drawback of the I-O approach is that it captures only one side of the story. If investment in the oil and gas (or manufacturing) industry comes at the expense of investment in other sectors, then the employment and output effects of the investment alternative must be scored against the oil and gas figures. Likewise, if new oil and gas employees are hired away from other sectors, then their previous incomes, and the induced jobs they supported, must be subtracted as well. And if an increase in US oil and gas production substantially lowers the US energy trade deficit, real dollar appreciation—either through inflation or nominal exchange rate adjustment—could reduce the economic competitiveness of some manufacturing industries. Theory suggests that if the economy is at full employment, these factors will result in a net increase in jobs and output that is either zero or considerably lower than the gross estimates I-O models provide. We have criticized green jobs proponents in the past (as have fossil fuel industry analysts) for using gross rather than net estimates of the economic and employment gains of clean energy investments (Houser, Mohan, and Hoffman 2010). The same criticism applies to the Wood Mackenzie, IHS CERA, McKinsey, and ACC studies referenced above.

If there is surplus labor and capital sitting on the sidelines, as is the case today, then other considerations apply. New investment in oil and gas production is less likely to ration capital away from other sectors through higher interest rates. High levels of unemployment mean that demand for workers in the oil patch is unlikely to translate into broad-based wage inflation. Exchange rate effects could still come into play, but as we have argued in the context of cap-and-trade legislation, as long as the economy is operating below its potential, more of the economic and employment benefits that I-O models suggest are likely to be achieved (Houser, Mohan, and Hoffman 2010). The IHS CERA, Wood Mackenzie, and ACC reports, however, look out over a 20- to 25-year time horizon, by which point hopefully the US economy will be back near full employment. So a broader macroeconomic analysis is required to assess the true net effects of growing US oil and gas supply.

Citigroup's commodities research division took a crack at such an analysis as part of its spring 2012 report on future US oil and gas production potential (Morse et al. 2012). As discussed in chapter 3, the group has one of the more optimistic supply outlooks and expects considerable efficiency-driven reductions in demand as well. Using a proprietary macroeconomic model, Citigroup assessed the net economic and employment effects of these combined supply and demand projections in 2020. While as a commercial analysis, the methodological description in the report is somewhat limited, the authors describe the model as including exchange rate, interest rate, and wage rate effects.

In comparing its supply and demand projections against a baseline with "standard decline rates for US hydrocarbon production as well as more modest declines in consumption," Citigroup finds a 2 to 3.3 percent increase in GDP and up to 3.6 million additional jobs in 2020. Its analysis includes a fairly modest 1.6 to 5.4 percent real appreciation in the dollar, and thus a reduction in net energy imports that is greater than the resulting increase in imports of other goods and services. Crude prices fall by 16.1 percent in the supply growth scenario relative to its base case assumptions.

The limitation of the Citigroup study is its timeframe and scope of coverage. The report assesses the effects of increased oil and gas supply only through 2020, a period in which the authors expect the economy to be operating below full employment. The report acknowledges that much of the economic and employment gains they forecast for 2020 will be offset by general equilibrium effects as the economy returns to full employment but do not quantify the net long-term economic effect. Neither the Citigroup study nor the ACC, Wood Mackenzie, McKinsey, or IHS CERA reports include detailed modeling of the energy market effects of increased oil and gas supply, including the effects on electricity prices, renewable energy generation, and coal demand.

Our Approach

Our analysis builds on the above studies in several ways. Like Citibank we model the net economic effects of prospective oil and gas supply growth rather than looking at the gross effect alone, as in the case of the IHS CERA, McKinsey, Wood Mackenzie, and ACC studies. That requires isolating the economic effect of the shock of higher natural gas and oil production currently unfolding. As described in chapter 3, we do this by comparing three scenarios—pre-shale, conservative, and optimistic—in which all we change are assumptions about resource availability and access.

We model our scenarios using the Energy Information Administration (EIA) National Energy Modeling System (NEMS), which combines a US econometric dynamic equilibrium growth model developed by IHS Global Insight (and used in the IHS CERA study to assess the indirect effects of unconventional oil and gas production) with a US energy system model that EIA developed and maintains. NEMS is unique in the detail in which it evaluates the energy sector effects of changes in price, supply, and demand. The IHS Global Insight model, which is part of the NEMS macroeconomic activity module (MAM), encompasses over 1,700 variables covering final demands, aggregate supply, prices, incomes, international trade, industrial detail, interest rates, and financial flows. Built on the Wharton econometric forecasting model, the IHS Global Insight model combines insights from a variety of theoretical concepts—Keynesian, neoclassical, monetarist, supply-side, and rational expectations—with a goal of ensuring that short-run cyclical developments fit well with a robust framework for long-term equilibrium growth (EIA 2011e). The model captures improvements in long-term economic growth potential from increased energy supply (treated as a factor of production) as well as changes in short-term economic growth from greater energy investment and lower energy prices.

The MAM uses the energy production, consumption, and price estimates from the other NEMS modules to project macroeconomic outcomes. These macroeconomic variables are in turn are used by other NEMS modules to forecast energy market developments. This communication is conducted through an integrating module, a sort of control panel that executes other NEMS modules to ensure energy market equilibrium in each projection year. The solution methodology is based on the Gauss-Seidel algorithm. The model starts with an initial solution, then runs each NEMS module to arrive at a new solution. That solution becomes the new starting point and the process repeats itself until the model reaches a user-defined convergence threshold. By connecting the MAM with the other parts of NEMS through the integrating module, the model allows us to robustly assess the macroeconomic effect of changes in US oil and gas supply, capturing feedback loops within the energy sector from changes in GDP growth, industrial output, trade, and employment (see appendix A for more detail).

We make one major enhancement to NEMS for this analysis. As currently configured, energy sector investment demand in the MAM is determined by changes in energy prices rather than production quantities. So if oil prices rise, upstream oil and gas investment demand rises as well. If prices fall, investment demand falls alongside them. This works relatively well for small-scale market changes, but less well for a shock as large as the current oil and gas boom. As structured, a dramatic increase in US oil and gas production due to newly accessible resources translates into a decrease in overall oil and gas investment. We improve the MAM's treatment of the current boom by estimating the increase in upstream oil and gas investment associated with our conservative and optimistic scenarios relative to the pre-shale scenarios outside of NEMS and adjusting upstream oil and gas investment demand in the MAM accordingly. To do this, we draw on the 2012 IHS CERA study, which included detailed estimates of the investment required to produce unconventional oil and gas (IHS CERA 2012). We multiply IHS CERA's per barrel and per cubic foot oil and natural gas investment estimates by the difference in production between our pre-shale and our conservative and optimistic scenarios to estimate the additional investment required to achieve the production increases associated with each scenario. These investment estimates are calculated endogenously in the model and added to the baseline upstream oil and gas investment demand projections in the MAM. As the model converges, it captures the macroeconomic effect of this increase in investment demand, including higher demand for the goods and services needed to produce oil and gas, as well as increased competition for capital in other sectors due to higher interest rates. We have taken a similar approach in the past to assess the macroeconomic effect of power sector investment changes under cap-and-trade legislation (Houser, Mohan, and Hoffman 2010).

Macroeconomic Results

The recent and projected increase in US oil and gas production shapes the country's economic outlook in several ways. New investment is required to bring that production online, which creates demand for labor and materials. Higher production means lower prices, which reduce business costs and increase real household income. Higher production also means lower oil and gas imports, which change the country's international trade position. The net effect of these factors on overall economic growth is complex, and varies over time.

Investment

Oil and gas are an important source of investment demand in the United States, ranking third behind manufacturing and finance and insurance in total private nonresidential fixed asset investment in 2011. The unconventional boom has made the sector even more important after the financial crisis, accounting for 41 percent of nonresidential private investment growth between 2009 and 2011.

Using investment cost estimates from the 2012 IHS CERA report, our conservative and optimistic scenarios require an additional $29 billion and $95 billion, respectively, in annual oil and gas investment (in 2005 chained dollars), between 2013 and 2035 relative to the pre-shale scenario. That investment shock creates demand for construction materials, capital goods, and professional services, from engineering contractors to drilling rigs to the steel and cement used in the drilling and well completion process. Upstream oil and gas itself is not terribly labor intensive, but many of its supporting industries are, leading to indirect effects in the form of an increase in employment alongside the increase in investment. When those workers use their paychecks to buy food, clothing, and entertainment, additional induced economic activity is created.

Producer Revenue

Revenue earned once new oil and gas wells start producing has additional economic effects. Domestic oil and gas output combined is 19 percent and 54 percent higher in the conservative and optimistic scenarios, respectively, between 2013 and 2035 compared with the pre-shale scenario, but revenue is up by only 7 and 19 percent. This is because prices decline in the face of increased supply. In the pre-shale scenario, Henry Hub natural gas prices average $7.40 per million British thermal units (MMBtu) (in real 2010 US dollars) between 2013 and 2035. In the conservative case prices fall to an average of $5.44 per

Figure 4.2   Difference in annual energy producer revenue, 2013–35 annual average

billions of 2010 dollars

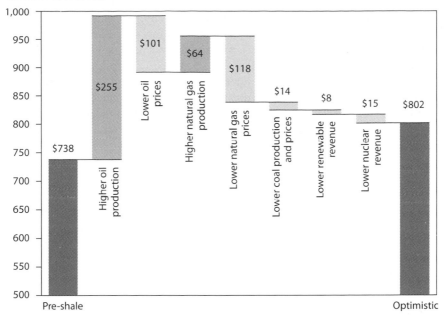

Source: Authors' calculations.

MMBtu, a modest increase from the $4 per MMBtu average in 2011, but one in line with futures prices as of mid-year 2013. Prices in the optimistic case average $3.12 per MMBtu through 2035. This means natural gas producers actually see a net decline in revenue of between $17 billion and $54 billion per year on average between 2013 and 2035 compared with the pre-shale case.

Oil prices fall considerably less than natural gas prices in our analysis. The natural gas production delta between our pre-shale and conservative and optimistic scenarios between 2013 and 2035 is 11 billion to 26 billion cubic feet per day (Bcfd). That is 16 percent to 37 percent the size of the total North American natural gas market in 2012, a big increase in overall supply. In contrast, the 1.5 million and 5.3 million barrels per day (bbl/d) average increase in US oil production in the conservative and optimistic cases between 2013 and 2035 is only a respective 2 percent and 6 percent increase above current global oil supply, and 1.5 to 5 percent above projected oil supply during that period. As a result, in our analysis crude oil prices are 3 percent lower in the conservative scenario and 11 percent lower in the optimistic scenario between 2013 and 2035. This leaves oil producers with a $54 billion to $154 billion increase in annual production revenue relative to the pre-shale case (figure 4.2).

Predicting the effects of increased oil production on global oil prices is much tougher than the same analysis for natural gas because of the Organization of Petroleum Exporting Countries (OPEC). The NEMS assumes a long-term oil price elasticity of 0.25, based on historical experience and the academic literature. In the face of rising US production, however, OPEC could curb investment to defend current prices, as the cartel did successfully when demand collapsed in the wake of the 2008 financial crisis. This would lead to smaller price reductions than the model estimates. However, increased US production in the face of soft global demand also could undermine OPEC cohesion, with members attempting to shore up revenue by producing above their quota. If this occurs, as it did in the mid-1980s, price reductions could be even greater than our analysis suggests. This topic warrants considerable new research and analysis, but as there are significant risks and uncertainties on both sides, we think the price reductions in the model are a reasonable best guess.

Lower oil and gas prices mean higher oil and gas demand, and thus lower demand for other energy sources. We estimate a $16 billion to $37 billion per year decrease in coal, nuclear, and renewable energy production revenue in the conservative and optimistic cases, respectively, between 2013 and 2035 (figure 4.2). On net, energy producer revenue increases by $22 billion per year in the conservative scenario and $64 billion per year in the optimistic scenario (tables 4.1 and 4.2).

Energy Expenditures

While the decrease in prices resulting from increased US oil and gas supply is bad news for energy producers, it is an economic windfall for energy consumers. The country's annual energy bill falls by $56 billion on average between 2013 and 2035 in the conservative scenario and $177 billion in the optimistic case (tables 4.1 and 4.2), and that is accounting for the increase in demand that occurs due to lower prices, known as the rebound effect. Oil expenditures fall by more than natural gas expenditures despite a smaller change in price—$75 billion versus $53 billion in the optimistic case (see figure 4.3). The country spends much more on oil than it does on natural gas, and the rebound effect is greater in gas thanks to coal-gas fuel switching in the power sector. Since natural gas sets the price of electricity in many parts of the country, annual power expenditures fall significantly as well: by $40 billion on average between 2013 and 2035 in the optimistic case.

By sector, the biggest savings occur in transportation and industrial sectors where oil and gas consumption is highest (figure 4.4). For energy-intensive industries this means lower production costs, increased international competitiveness, and lower product prices for consumers. The residential and commercial sectors see impressive savings as well—a combined $57 billion per year in the optimistic scenario, thanks primarily to lower electricity prices. Add residential energy expenditures to the share of transport energy expenditures attributable to passenger vehicles and the average household saves between

Table 4.1 Energy prices, revenue, and expenditures, by scenario, 2013–20

Sector	Pre-shale Value	Conservative Value	Conservative Difference (percent)	Optimistic Value	Optimistic Difference (percent)
Energy prices					
Oil (2010 US dollars per barrel)	115.40	112.50	−2.5	104.70	−9.3
Gasoline (2010 US dollars per gallon)	3.62	3.56	−1.7	3.35	−7.5
Natural gas (2010 US dollars per MMBtu)	5.47	4.31	−21.2	2.77	−49.3
Coal (2010 US dollars per short ton)[a]	41.10	41.00	−0.4	41.30	0.4
Electricity (2010 cents per kWh)	9.98	9.63	−3.5	9.04	−9.4
Producer revenue					
Oil (billions of 2010 US dollars)	351	390	11.0	453	29.1
Natural gas (billions of 2010 US dollars)	107	95	−11.2	72	−32.3
Coal (billions of 2010 US dollars)	45	42	−7.4	42	−7.9
Nuclear (billions of 2010 US dollars)	51	48	−5.7	42	−16.5
Renewables (billions of 2010 US dollars)	92	86	−6.7	77	−16.2
Energy expenditures					
Economywide (billions of 2010 US dollars)	1,438	1,403	−2.4	1,322	−8.1
Household (2010 US dollars per home)	5,377	5,263	−2.1	4,987	−7.3

kWh = kilowatt hour; MMBtu = millions of British thermal units

a. Includes both thermal coal used in power generation and more expensive metallurgical coal used in steel making. Average coal prices are lower in the optimistic scenario than in the conservative scenario because the thermal/metallurgical ratio has declined.

Source: Authors' calculations using the National Energy Modeling System.

$159 and $513 per year in energy costs between 2013 and 2035, making money available to save or spend on other goods and services.

The EIA's 2012 and 2013 outlooks both forecast a decline in energy expenditures as a share of GDP from current levels. This is also true in all three of our scenarios (figure 4.5). In the pre-shale case, energy expenditures fall from 9.1 percent of GDP in 2011 to 6.8 percent by 2035. In the conservative scenario, energy expenditures fall to 6.3 percent of GDP. In the optimistic case, they fall to 5.6 percent. On average, there is 1 percent of GDP difference in energy costs between the pre-shale and optimistic scenarios between 2013 and 2035.

Over the past couple of years, the consumer benefit of the oil and gas boom has likely been greater than these long-term projections suggest. Between 2008 and 2012 the United States accounted for more than half of global oil production growth (figure 4.6). That helped restrain global oil prices at a time when North Sea production was falling and markets were plagued by a host of supply disruptions, from Sudan to Syria to sanctions against Iran. As men-

Table 4.2 Energy prices, revenue, and expenditures, by scenario, 2021–35

Sector	Pre-shale Value	Conservative Value	Conservative Difference (percent)	Optimistic Value	Optimistic Difference (percent)
Energy prices					
Oil (2010 US dollars per barrel)	129.10	124.60	–3.5	114.60	–11.2
Gasoline (2010 US dollars per gallon)	3.99	3.92	–1.8	3.61	–9.6
Natural gas (2010 US dollars per MMBtu)	8.43	6.04	–28.4	3.31	–60.8
Coal (2010 US dollars per short ton)[a]	46.70	46.00	–1.5	45.70	–2.2
Electricity (2010 cents per kWh)	10.51	9.80	–6.7	8.85	–15.8
Producer revenue					
Oil (billions of 2010 US dollars)	388	451	16.4	572	47.6
Natural gas (billions of 2010 US dollars)	164	146	–11.0	101	–38.4
Coal (billions of 2010 US dollars)	58	52	–9.3	39	–31.5
Nuclear (billions of 2010 US dollars)	65	55	–15.0	46	–29.8
Renewables (billions of 2010 US dollars)	127	110	–13.1	95	–25.2
Energy expenditures					
Economywide (billions of 2010 US dollars)	1,656	1,588	–4.1	1,446	–12.7
Household (2010 US dollars per home)	5,294	5,112	–3.4	4,716	–10.9

kWh = kilowatt hour; MMBtu = millions of British thermal units

a. Includes both thermal coal used in power generation and more expensive metallurgical coal used in steel making. Average coal prices are lower in the optimistic scenario than in the conservative scenario because the thermal/metallurgical ratio has declined.

Source: Authors' calculations using the National Energy Modeling System.

tioned above, quantifying exactly how much increased US output mitigated the price effects of these disruptions is a challenge. Had the United States produced less, other countries may well have produced more.

That said, spare capacity in Gulf Cooperation Council countries—the OPEC members most likely to increase output to help supply the market—was already running pretty low in 2012 as Saudi Arabia increased production to replace Iranian supply curtailed by sanctions. In that time period, others could not have replaced the full 2.2 million bbl/d of US production growth, on par with total Iranian exports before sanctions went into effect. Prices would have needed to rise to balance the market. For oil, short-term price elasticity is considerably lower than long-term price elasticity, so the required market-balancing price increase could have been substantial. That could well have been too much for a fragile US economic recovery to handle.

Figure 4.3   Annual average difference in energy expenditures by source, 2013–35

billions of 2010 dollars

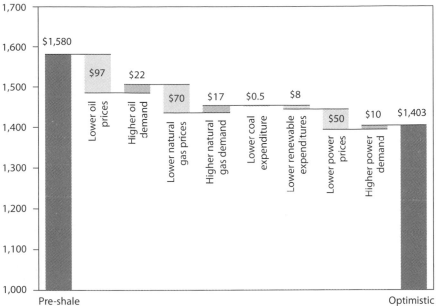

Source: Authors' calculations.

Oil and Gas as Economic Stimulus

Simply summing up the direct, indirect, and induced effects of the investment, production revenue, and cost savings discussed above—the approach most existing studies take—overstates the effect of the current oil and gas boom on overall economic growth. Greater demand for investment and labor in oil, gas, and supporting industries puts upward pressure on interest rates and wages, which reduces investment and employment in other parts of the economy. Higher domestic prices mean a stronger real exchange rate, even if the nominal exchange rate remains unchanged, which can offset some or all of the improvement in the current account balance that decreased oil imports create.

But, when the economy is operating below full employment, these equilibrium effects are less pronounced. And in the IHS Global Insight model used in this analysis, the economy does not return to full employment in the pre-shale scenario for several years. Against this backdrop, the current oil and gas boom acts as a relatively potent economic stimulus, combining upstream investment (akin to infrastructure spending) with energy cost savings (akin to tax cuts). In our analysis, US GDP is between 0.6 percent (conservative) and 2.1 percent

Figure 4.4   Annual average difference in energy expenditures by sector, 2013–35

billions of 2010 dollars

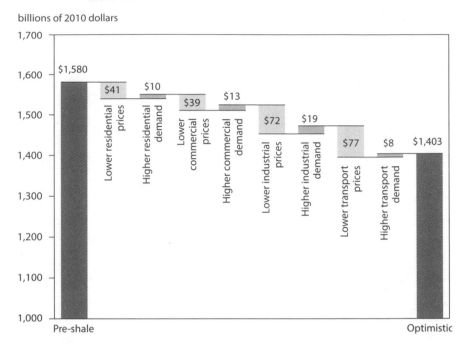

Source: Authors' calculations.

(optimistic) higher on average between 2013 and 2020 due to the oil and gas boom (table 4.3).[2] That is an increase in the average annual growth rate of 0.09 to 0.19 percent. Total employment is between 0.5 and 1.8 percent higher, an addition of 0.8 million to 2.5 million jobs, thanks to a combination of higher overall output and a shift in the composition of economic output in a more labor-intensive direction. That takes the average unemployment rate between 2013 and 2020 down by 0.6 percent in the optimistic case.

The magnitude of the boom's short-term economic effect is on par with the American Recovery and Reinvestment Act. The Congressional Budget Office (CBO) estimates that the Recovery Act added between 0.3 and 1.9 percent to average US GDP between 2009 and 2013 (figure 4.7) and increased total

---

2. As energy is considered a factor of production in the IHS Global Insight model, greater oil and gas supply increases potential GDP between 2013 and 2020 by an average of 1 percent in the optimistic scenario (table 4.3). Most of the short-term increase in GDP and employment, however, comes from the simulative demand-side effect of both greater investment and real consumption—thanks to lower energy costs—that accelerate the economy's return to full employment. While the difference in potential GDP between 2013 and 2020 between the pre-shale and optimistic scenarios is 1 percent, the difference in actual GDP is 2.1 percent.

Figure 4.5 Energy expenditures as a share of GDP, 1970–2035

percent

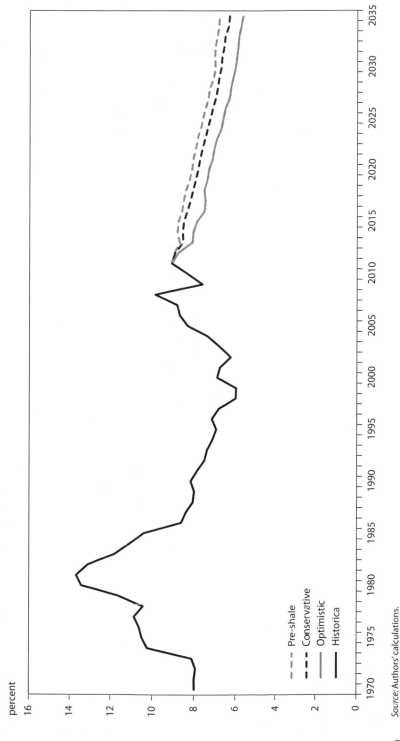

- - - Pre-shale
- - - Conservative
Optimistic
Historica

Source: Authors' calculations.

Figure 4.6 Change in oil production, 2012 versus 2008

thousand barrels per day

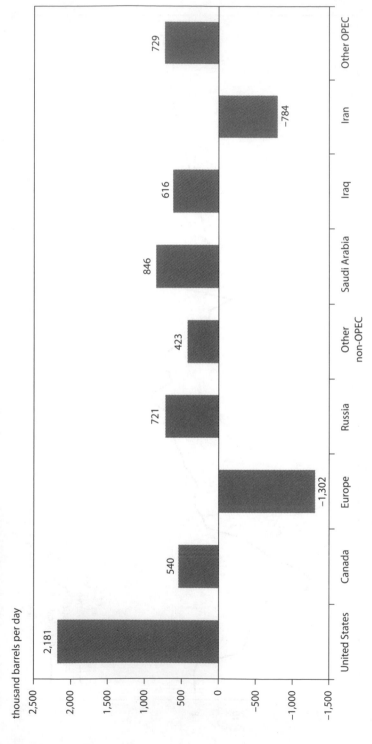

OPEC = Organization of Petroleum Exporting Countries

Source: IEA (2013a).

Table 4.3 Macroeconomic impact, by scenario, 2013–20

	Pre-shale	Conservative		Optimistic	
			Difference		**Difference**
Indicator	**Value**	**Value**	(percent)	**Value**	(percent)
Output					
Real GDP (billions of 2005 chained US dollars)	15,293	15,389	0.6	15,620	2.1
Potential GDP (billions of 2005 chained US dollars)	16,526	16,571	0.3	16,687	1.0
Real GDP growth (percent per year)	2.65	2.74	3.4	2.84	7.0
Employment					
Nonfarm employment (millions)	141.30	142.10	0.5	143.80	1.8
Unemployment rate (percent)	7.40	7.20	−2.4	6.80	−8.2
Prices					
Consumer price index (1982–84 = 100)	2.51	2.50	−0.3	2.50	−0.4
AA corporate bond (percent, nominal)	6.70	6.80	0.5	6.90	2.6
Hourly compensation (1992 = 1.0)	1.18	1.18	0.1	1.19	0.9

Source: Authors' calculations using the National Energy Modeling System.

Figure 4.7 Differences in average annual GDP and employment

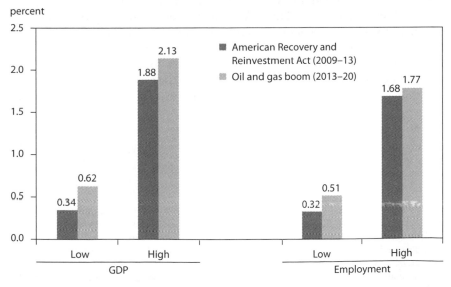

Note: Low and high estimates from the Congressional Budget Office for the American Recovery and Reinvestment Act versus authors' conservative and optimistic scenarios used in this analysis.

Sources: CBO (2012); authors' calculations.

employment by 0.3 to 1.7 percent (CBO 2012). There are a couple of caveats to keep in mind when considering these findings, however. First, the 2012 NEMS version of the IHS Global Insight model used for this analysis is relatively pessimistic about the pace of the economic recovery, with the United States not returning to full employment until shortly after 2020. In the 2013 version of the model, the United States reaches full employment in 2020. The CBO projects the US economy will return to full employment in 2017 (CBO 2013). Second, Recovery Act stimulus was broadly spread throughout the country while the oil and gas boom is more concentrated. This means that in oil- and gas-producing areas, prices will likely rise faster than our nationwide analysis suggests. It is already happening in places like North Dakota, where the inflation rate is much higher than in the rest of the country due to booming production in the Bakken. Our model does not capture this well. Should the economy recover faster than the baseline IHS Global Insight projections, the effect of increased oil and gas production on short-term economic growth and job creation will be lower than the estimates outlined above. Regardless, the boom could not come at a better time economically, as the Recovery Act stimulus tapers off and the prospects for additional fiscal support for the economy look dim.

Long-Term Economic Effects

Beyond 2020 the economic benefits of the oil and gas boom are more limited. As the economy returns to full employment, interest rates rise and labor costs increase beyond oil- and gas-producing areas. In our analysis, AA corporate bond rates are 5.3 percent higher between 2021 and 2035 in the optimistic scenario than in the pre-shale case, and hourly labor costs are 5.4 percent higher (table 4.4). This takes the rate of economic growth back to pre-shale levels.[3] The economy keeps the gains it made between 2013 and 2020, however. Increased oil and gas supply shifts the US economic production frontier (potential GDP) out by 1.3 percent in the optimistic case and actual GDP by 1 percent on average between 2021 and 2035. But this is a one-time positive shock to the economy, not a sustained increase in the rate of economic growth.

The situation is very different from the information technology (IT) boom of the 1990s, which is often cited as a precedent for today's growth in oil and gas supply. According to growth economists Dale Jorgenson and Mun Ho,

---

3. The 2012 IHS CERA study also highlights the importance of general equilibrium considerations when assessing the long-term economic effects of the unconventional oil and gas boom. "By 2035," it states, "we have estimated almost 3.5 million jobs will be supported by unconventional oil and natural gas activity. However, one cannot say that in 2035 3.5 million workers would have been added to the unemployment rolls if unconventional oil and natural gas did not exist. If unconventional oil and natural gas did not exist, the population and labor force size would still be the same and those workers would have found work in other sectors of the economy."

Table 4.4 Macroeconomic impact, by scenario, 2021–35

Indicator	Pre-shale Value	Conservative Value	Conservative Difference (percent)	Optimistic Value	Optimistic Difference (percent)
Output					
Real GDP (billions of 2005 chained US dollars)	20,653	20,729	0.4	20,866	1.0
Potential GDP (billions of 2005 chained US dollars)	21,517	21,613	0.4	21,796	1.3
Real GDP growth (percent per year)	2.59	2.58	−0.5	2.56	−1.1
Employment					
Nonfarm employment (millions)	157.80	158.20	0.3	158.80	0.6
Unemployment rate (percent)	5.60	5.60	0.6	5.70	2.4
Prices					
Consumer price index (1982–84 = 100)	3.20	3.22	0.6	3.29	2.8
AA corporate bond (percent, nominal)	7.40	7.50	1.6	7.80	5.3
Hourly compensation (1992 = 1.0)	1.41	1.43	1.5	1.49	5.4

Source: Authors' calculations using the National Energy Modeling System.

IT-producing industries, both equipment and services, accounted for 3 percent of US economic output between 1995 and 2000, on par with the oil and gas sector going forward (Jorgenson, Ho, and Samuels 2010). But the output of IT-producing industries was not the game changer for the US economy; it was the productivity improvements that IT equipment and services made possible in other parts of the economy. By installing increasingly inexpensive hardware and software, companies could produce more output with less labor and capital, driving down product prices. IT also made entirely new types of business activity possible, from just-in-time manufacturing to online dating. Jorgenson, Ho, and Samuels estimate that IT-consuming industries—those for which more than 15 percent of the capital input is IT—accounted for more than half of the growth in US economic output between 1995 and 2000.

Energy sector developments have had transformative effects in the past. The switch from wood to coal as the predominant source of energy supply in the United States enabled new types of industrial activity because coal contained much more energy by volume and was thus easier to transport. The widespread deployment of electric power generation had a transformative effect as well: Electricity is much more versatile and flexible than raw fossil fuels (Stern 2011). But the current oil and gas boom does not yield a different and more convenient form of energy; it provides more of the same energy at a lower price. That is certainly helpful, as evidenced by the outward shift in US potential GDP discussed above, but it is not transformative in the same way that IT was in the 1990s.

Implications for the Trade Balance and Exchange Rate

Growth in domestic oil and natural gas production has already significantly reduced US dependence on imported energy, and in both our conservative and optimistic scenarios, that decline continues for the next couple decades. In the conservative case, net energy imports as a share of total primary energy consumption decline from 18.3 percent in 2011 to 14.6 percent in 2020 and 11.7 percent in 2035 (figure 4.8 and table 4.5). In the optimistic case, net imports decline to 7.4 percent of consumption by 2020 and 1.7 percent by 2035—levels not seen since the 1950s. This contrasts starkly with the pre-shale scenario, where net imports stay between 16 and 20 percent of total energy consumption through 2035.

That the United States does not become a net energy exporter in the optimistic scenario, despite following a production pathway similar to the more ambitious Citigroup and Wood Mackenzie forecasts, is the result of changes on the demand side of the energy equation. Lower prices and faster economic growth lead to a 2.3 percent increase in overall energy demand in 2035 relative to the pre-shale scenario (table 4.5). Efficiency policy can counteract this rebound effect, as discussed in chapter 5. A lower energy trade deficit in quantity terms means a lower deficit in value terms as well. In our pre-shale scenario, the US energy trade deficit grows from roughly $330 billion today (in real 2010 US dollars) to nearly $430 billion by 2035 (table 4.5). In our conservative scenario, net energy imports stay roughly flat, averaging $335 billion per year in real 2010 dollars between 2013 and 2035, thanks to both smaller import quantities and lower prices. In the optimistic case, real net energy imports decline sharply, falling to $116 billion by 2035. As a share of GDP, net US energy imports fall to 1.2 percent by 2035 in the conservative scenario and 0.4 percent in the optimistic case, a 0.4 and 1.2 percentage point reduction, respectively, from the pre-shale case (figure 4.9).

Changes in the US energy trade balance significantly improve the country's terms of trade, that is, the price of US imports relative to exports. Terms of trade in developed economies have declined over the past decade, in large part because of rising oil prices (IMF 2011). The current oil and gas boom helps correct this for the United States by both reducing oil import quantities and lowering global oil prices. Improved terms of trade create a wealth effect, which is captured in the headline macroeconomic results reported earlier in this chapter.

A lower energy trade deficit, however, does not necessarily lead to a lower trade deficit overall. The Netherlands experienced a natural gas boom in the 1960s following the discovery of significant hydrocarbon resources in the North Sea. This significantly improved the country's energy trade balance, but also led to an appreciation in the guilder, which made the country's manufacturing exports less competitive. This phenomenon came to be known as Dutch

Figure 4.8 Net imports as a share of total energy consumption, 1949–2035

percent

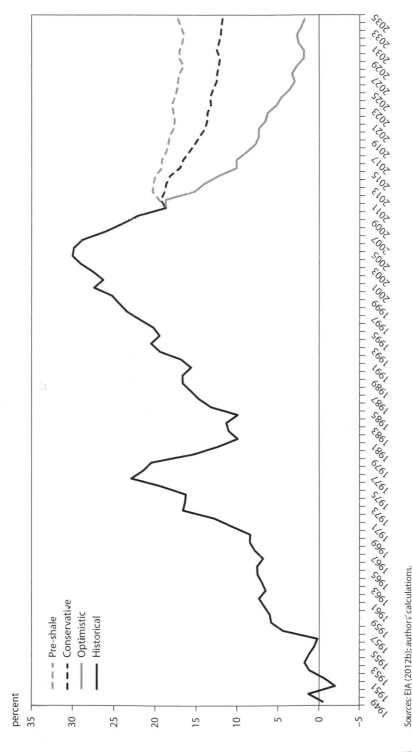

Sources: EIA (2012b); authors' calculations.

Table 4.5 Energy trade balance, by scenario, 2020, 2030, and 2035

Source	Pre-shale			Conservative			Optimistic		
	2020	2030	2035	2020	2030	2035	2020	2030	2035
Quantity									
Crude oil (million barrels/day)	-8.10	-8.20	-9.30	-7.20	-7.20	-7.60	-4.60	-3.40	-3.70
Refined products (billion barrels/day)	-0.15	-0.06	-0.08	0.12	0.24	0.35	0.52	0.86	1.01
Natural gas (trillion cubic feet)	-4.10	-2.00	-1.20	-1.00	2.50	3.70	0.70	6.00	7.00
Coal (million short tons)	64.50	49.90	70.70	67.00	81.50	93.70	79.70	86.90	95.60
Biofuels (million barrels/day)	-0.01	-0.04	-0.10	0.00	-0.02	-0.03	0.01	-0.02	-0.03
All energy sources (quadrillion British thermal units)	-18.00	-17.70	-18.20	-14.50	-12.60	-12.50	-7.40	-2.00	-1.90
Total energy consumption (quadrillion British thermal units)	98.50	103.80	106.00	99.40	104.10	106.80	100.20	105.60	108.40
Net import share (percent)	18.30	17.10	17.20	14.60	12.10	11.70	7.40	1.80	1.70
Value (billions of real 2010 US dollars)									
Crude oil	-356.00	-394.50	-446.10	-303.00	-330.50	-367.50	-179.00	-143.70	-165.90
Refined products	5.30	11.30	13.00	7.90	15.00	20.40	8.80	19.30	25.30
Natural gas	-8.40	-5.20	-4.50	-1.50	5.10	9.40	0.80	7.00	9.80
Coal	10.00	8.60	12.60	10.40	14.20	16.70	12.10	14.80	16.90
Biofuels	-0.30	-1.20	-3.70	0.00	-0.80	-1.90	0.20	-0.60	-1.60
All energy sources	-349.50	-381.10	-428.80	-286.20	-297.00	-322.90	-157.20	-103.20	-115.60
Share of GDP (percent)	-1.90	-1.60	-1.60	-1.50	-1.20	-1.20	-0.80	-0.40	-0.40

Source: Authors' calculations using the National Energy Modeling System.

Figure 4.9 Energy trade balance as a share of GDP, 1970–2035

percent

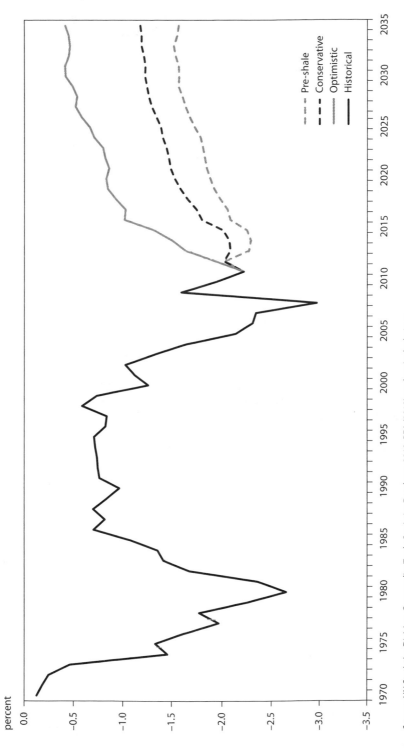

Sources: UN Statistics Division, Commodity Trade Statistics Database, 2012; BEA (2013); authors' calculations.

disease;[4] it has appeared elsewhere since and works as follows. A country makes a major natural resource discovery, leading to a surge in investment in its natural resource sector. If the country is smaller and the investment comes primarily from abroad, the increased inflow of foreign exchange increases the country's money supply. If the country's exchange rate is fixed, domestic prices then rise. If the exchange rate is flexible, nominal appreciation results. In either case, the real exchange rate strengthens (Corden 1984). In a larger country where most of the investment comes from domestic sources, the increase in investment and labor demand from the resource sector also pushes up prices, leading to real exchange rate appreciation as well. A stronger real exchange rate makes nonresource exports less competitive, leading to a decline in the country's manufacturing trade balance. Some economists argue that manufacturing sector investment produces more long-term productivity gains than resource investment, and Dutch disease thus reduces potential GDP growth.

A 2010 IMF review of the literature finds strong empirical evidence that natural resource shocks—either big new discoveries or big price increases—result in exchange rate appreciation, reallocation of production factors (labor and capital) away from manufacturing, and lower net exports (or higher net imports) of manufactured goods (Magud and Sosa 2010). This appears consistent with the Canadian, Brazilian, and Australian experience over the past decade: All three countries have seen a boom in natural resource exports, real effective exchange rate appreciation, and a decline in their manufacturing trade balance.

Likewise, in our modeling, the long-term increase in labor and capital costs resulting from a surge in oil and gas investment (table 4.4) results in real dollar appreciation, even though the nominal exchange rate is fixed in our analysis, and leads to a deterioration in the country's nonenergy trade balance that offsets much of the improved energy trade position. Of course, a number of factors led to the recent declines in Canada's, Australia's, and Brazil's manufacturing trade balance other than their domestic resource booms (e.g., China's entry into the World Trade Organization). Likewise, a number of characteristics of the current US oil and gas boom could help keep Dutch disease at bay.

The shale revolution has created a disconnect between US and international natural gas prices that will help offset the competitiveness effect of a stronger dollar for some energy-intensive industries. As the global reserve currency, the US dollar often behaves differently than other currencies under the same set of macroeconomic conditions. Also, a shift in where the money goes when Americans fill up at the pump—say, to ExxonMobil rather than Saudi Aramco—could affect domestic saving rates, which would affect the current account balance as well. An in-depth analysis of these factors is required to fully assess the effect of the current oil and gas boom on the US international economic position, and is outside the scope of this book. Our colleagues William Cline

---

4. Christine Ebrahim-zadeh, "Back to Basics," *Finance & Development* 40, no. 1, March 2003, www.imf.org/external/pubs/ft/fandd/2003/03/ebra.htm (accessed on September 8, 2013).

and John Williamson at the Peterson Institute for International Economics estimate that a 1 percent real appreciation of the dollar reduces the current account balance by 0.21 percent (Cline and Williamson 2011). We apply this rule of thumb to the 1.1 to 1.2 percent of GDP difference in the energy trade balance between our optimistic and pre-shale scenarios from 2020 to 2035 and estimate an upper-bound potential dollar appreciation of 5.7 percent, relatively modest by Canadian, Australian, or Brazilian standards. That assumes the current account balance remains constant. Should the current account balance decline, the effect on the dollar would be less. Chapter 6 explores how far lower-cost domestic energy might go in offsetting the impact of a potentially stronger exchange rate on US manufacturing competitiveness.

A More Resilient US Economy?

Increased domestic oil and gas investment and production are a potent economic stimulus in the short and medium term, improve US terms of trade, and modestly expand long-term economic output. But how effective are they in safeguarding the US economy from future energy price spikes? Even if the United States becomes a net oil exporter in the years ahead, domestic crude oil and refined product prices will almost certainly continue to track international prices. Gasoline prices in Canada, a net oil exporter, closely follow gasoline prices in the United States and international crude oil prices (figure 4.10). This is because both crude oil and refined products are internationally traded commodities with generally low transportation costs relative to shipment value, which creates a strong commercial incentive to arbitrage regional price differences.[5]

The above means that when there is a supply disruption in the Middle East, Canadian drivers take a hit alongside their peers in the United States. Increased domestic supply comes with economic benefits that can offset some of the cost of an oil price spike. If the US produced as much oil as it consumed and the price of crude increased from $100 to $130 per barrel because of a supply disruption in the Middle East, domestic oil and gas company profits and mineral royalties would increase by roughly the same amount as disposable household incomes decreased. These profits would either be distributed to shareholders or retained for future capital investment. But the consumer costs of oil price spikes fall hardest on the middle class, while the dividend benefits accrue disproportionately to the wealthy. Private royalty revenue falls somewhere in between (figures 4.11 and 4.12). Higher-income households save more and spend less than their middle- and lower-income counterparts

---

5. The rapid recent changes in North American supply have outpaced the construction of supporting pipeline capacity, leading to a relatively large gap between the price of crude oil produced in Alberta and the US midcontinent international crude price indexes, such as Brent, accounting for higher-cost nonpipeline transport options. But the prices still move in tandem and the industry is aggressively pursuing infrastructure investments that would close the price spread.

Figure 4.10 US and Canadian gasoline prices relative to international crude oil prices, 2000–12

US dollars (2005 = 100)

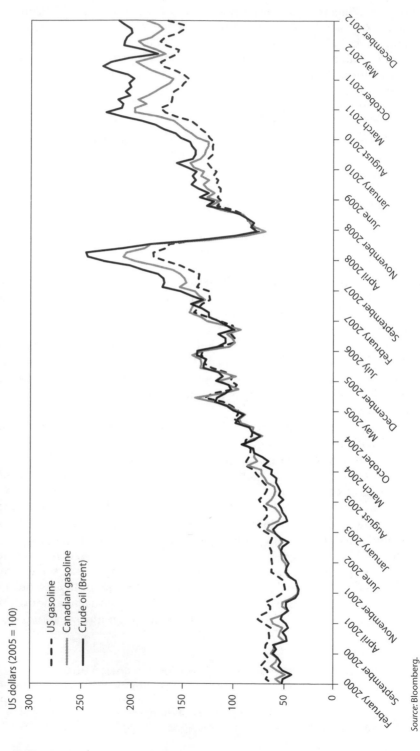

Source: Bloomberg.

Figure 4.11 Oil as a share of consumption expenditures, by annual income level, 2011

percent

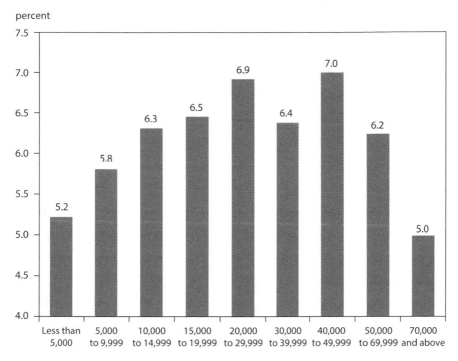

annual income in US dollars

Source: BLS (2013d).

(Huggett and Ventura 1995; Dynan, Skinner, and Zeldes 2004). That means higher dividend and royalty income would not offset the effect of higher oil prices on overall US consumption expenditures during an oil price spike, even if US oil supply equaled US oil demand.

The US oil and gas boom, however, lessens the effect of any particular international oil supply disruption on global oil prices. To the extent that US production is less volatile than Middle East production, changing the relative balance of the two in the global oil market makes the market as a whole less volatile. Tight oil production can be brought online quicker than complex conventional onshore or deepwater projects, so the unconventional boom could very well make global supply more price elastic, reducing the price effect of any given supply disruption. But given the importance of consumer spending in the US economy and the impact of oil price spikes on disposable consumer income, continued improvements in energy efficiency (discussed in the following chapter), particularly in the transportation sector, are an important complement to increased oil and gas supply.

Figure 4.12   Dividends as a share of adjusted income, by income level, 2010

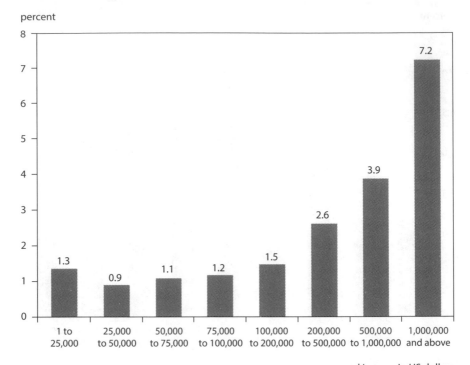

percent

annual income in US dollars

Source: IRS (2010).

5

Demand Side of the Ledger

While the recent boom in US oil and gas supply has attracted more attention, changes in US oil demand are playing an equally important role in transforming the country's energy landscape and reducing oil and gas imports. Indeed the sharp decline in US dependence on imported energy over the past few years, from 30 percent in 2005 to 16 percent in 2012, was driven more by a fall in energy demand rather than a rise in energy supply. In 2006 the Energy Information Administration (EIA) projected US energy production would grow by 1.5 percent per year between 2005 and 2012. Thanks primarily to an increase in oil and natural gas supply, it grew by 1.9 percent.

An even bigger surprise occurred on the demand side of the ledger. While the EIA projected 1.4 percent annual demand growth between 2005 and 2012, energy consumption declined by 0.7 percent a year. This change in demand accounted for 89 percent of the drop in US dependence on imported energy in 2012 relative to the EIA's 2006 outlook. This is true going forward as well: The EIA revised its projections upward for long-term US energy supply (2020–30) by 4 percent between 2006 and 2013, thanks primarily to the increase in domestic oil and gas production (EIA 2006, 2012c). But it revised its energy demand projections downward by 20 percent (figure 5.1).

Slower economic growth following the financial crisis explains most of the recent decline in US energy demand (figure 5.2). US GDP grew at an average annual rate of 3.1 percent between 1990 and 2005. The EIA in 2006 projected 3.1 percent annual growth through 2012. Instead, growth slowed to 1.1 percent on average per year. While this accounted for the majority of the change in demand (figure 5.2), accelerated energy efficiency improvements played an important role as well. Between 1990 and 2005 the amount of energy consumed per unit of GDP in the United States declined by 1.9 percent per year.

Figure 5.1 EIA projections for US primary energy consumption, 1970–2035

quadrillion British thermal units

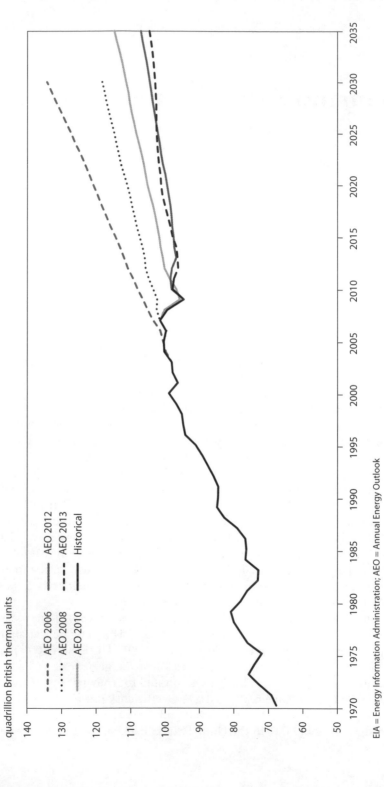

EIA = Energy Information Administration; AEO = Annual Energy Outlook

Sources: EIA (2006, 2008b, 2010b, 2012b, 2012c, 2013e).

Figure 5.2 Difference between projected and actual energy demand, 2012

quadrillion British thermal units

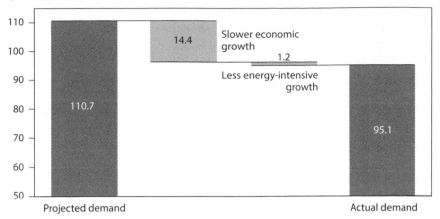

Note: Actual demand relative to the *2006 Annual Energy Outlook* projections.

Sources: EIA (2006, 2013d); BEA (2013).

Much of that decline was the result of a structural shift in the economy away from manufacturing to service sector activity (manufacturing uses more energy than services). Assuming much of the sectoral shift had run its course, in 2006 the EIA projected that annual energy-intensity improvements would slow to 1.7 percent between 2005 and 2012. Instead, the energy intensity of the economy fell by 2 percent per year.

Oil demand slowed even faster than energy demand as a whole. At 17.7 million barrels per day, US oil consumption[1] was 21 percent lower in 2012 than the EIA forecast in 2006, compared with a 14 percent downside surprise in energy demand overall. Slower economic growth accounts for much of this decline as well, but energy efficiency and fuel switching have played almost as great a role (figure 5.3). Improved fuel economy in vehicles, increased production of biofuels, and a switch from oil to natural gas in the chemicals industry have been particularly important in making the US economy less oil intensive.

Vehicle Efficiency

The oil price spike of the late 1970s led to the adoption of vehicle efficiency regulations in the United States known as corporate average fuel economy (CAFE) standards. CAFE standards set by the National Highway Traffic Safety

---

1. Includes natural gas liquids and refinery gains but excludes blending components such as biofuels.

Figure 5.3 Difference between projected and actual oil demand, 2012

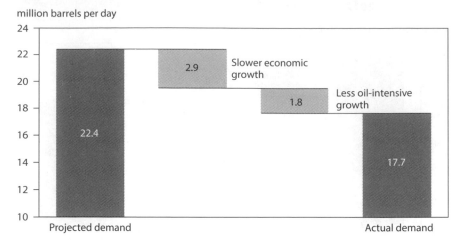

million barrels per day

Note: Actual demand relative to the *2006 Annual Energy Outlook* projections. Includes natural gas liquids and refinery gains but excludes blending components such as biofuels.

Sources: EIA (2006, 2013d); BEA (2013).

Administration (NHTSA), a part of the Department of Transportation, establish the average fuel efficiency, as measured in miles per gallon, that each automobile manufacturer's fleet must meet for each model year (MY). The standards for cars were raised from 18 miles per gallon (mpg) in 1978 to 27.5 mpg in 1985, but were left at that level for more than two decades as falling oil prices removed both the commercial and political pressure for energy-efficient vehicles (figure 5.4).

With oil prices once again on the rise Congress passed, and President Bush signed into law, the Energy Independence and Security Act of 2007 (EISA), which called on the NHTSA to increase CAFE standards for cars and light trucks combined to 35 mpg by 2020. In 2009, under the Obama administration, the NHTSA announced standards more aggressive than the EISA requirements: 34.1 mpg in 2016, 37.8 mpg for cars and 28.8 mpg for light trucks. These standards were harmonized with new greenhouse gas regulations for passenger vehicles announced by the US Environmental Protection Agency (EPA) at the same time.

As in the late 1970s, the MY2012–16 standards largely solidify trends already occurring in the market rather than forcing new behavior. As gasoline prices started to rise in 2002–03, so did the average efficiency of cars and light trucks purchased in the United States (figure 5.4). In 2000 the average fuel economy of new cars was 28.5 mpg. By 2007 the average mpg of new sales had risen to 31.2, before EISA was signed into law. Using the EIA's National Energy Modeling System, we estimate that high gasoline prices—between $3.50 and

Figure 5.4   Corporate average fuel economy (CAFE) standards and gasoline prices, 1955–2025

miles per gallon, weighted average new car sales

real 2012 US dollars per gallon

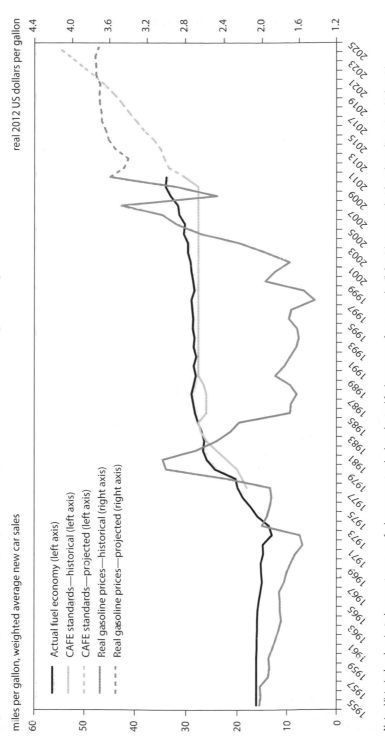

Note: Historical and projected corporate average fuel economy standards and actual fuel economy of new car sales (left axis) compared with real gasoline prices (right axis).

Sources: ORNL (2012); EPA and Department of Transportation (2012); EIA (2012b, 2012c); BLS (2013c).

Figure 5.5 Reduction in net oil imports by source, 2035

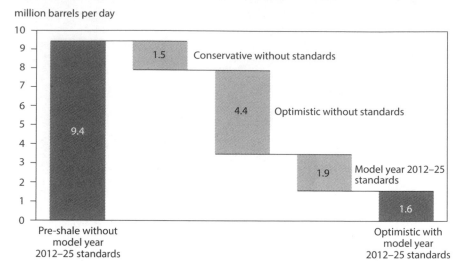

million barrels per day

Source: Authors' calculations using the National Energy Modeling System.

$4.00 a gallon over the next decade in 2010 dollars—will drive three-quarters of the fuel economy improvements mandated under the MY2012-16 standards.

In August 2012, however, the NHTSA and EPA released final CAFE/greenhouse gas standards for MY2017-25 vehicles. With a 55.3 mpg and 39.3 mpg target for cars and light trucks respectively by 2025, these standards go considerably beyond what high oil prices alone can deliver. In our pre-shale scenario, without the MY2012-25 standards, the United States imports 9.4 million barrels per day (bbl/d) of oil in 2035, up from 7.7 million bbl/d today. The increase in production in the conservative scenario reduces net oil imports by 1.5 million bbl/d (figure 5.5). Higher output in the optimistic case reduces net imports by another 4.4 million bbl/d. The MY2012-25 standards cut another 1.9 million bbl/d off the US oil import bill. This is enough to turn the United States into a net energy exporter in 2030 (figure 5.6).

The economic benefits of a fuel economy–driven reduction in US oil imports are a bit different from the benefits of increased supply discussed in chapter 4. More domestic oil output means more domestic investment, with its attendant supply chain effects, and lower oil prices. Improved efficiency can lower prices as well. Crude oil prices in our optimistic production scenario are 6 percent lower in 2035 with MY2012-25 CAFE standards than without, based on the same price elasticity, and thus the same uncertainties, as discussed in chapter 4. In our analysis, increased supply lowers prices by between 3 percent (conservative scenario) and 11 percent (optimistic scenario).

Vehicle efficiency has a much larger effect, however, on household oil expenditures than increased supply. Higher supply in the optimistic scenario

Figure 5.6　Net energy imports as a share of consumption with and without fuel economy standards, 1949–2035

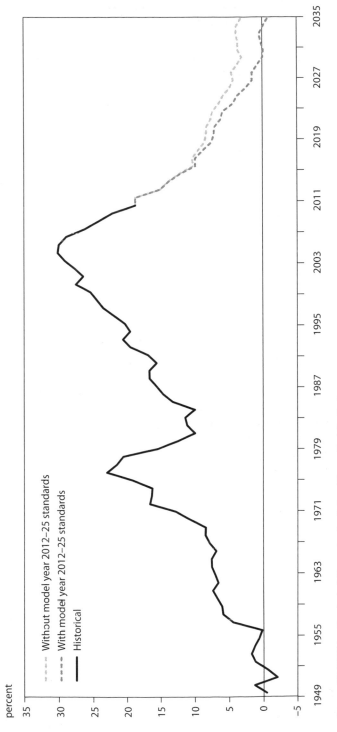

percent

Sources: EIA (2012b); authors' calculations using the National Energy Modeling System.

relative to the pre-shale case has nearly three times the effect on net US oil imports in 2035 as MY2012–25 standards (figure 5.5). Yet CAFE standards deliver nearly three times the savings to US drivers when they fill up their cars at the pump. This is because oil demand falls by 2.4 million bbl/d in 2035 due to MY2012–25 CAFE standards, whereas it increases by 670,000 bbl/d in response to increased domestic supply. More efficient vehicles cost more to buy, which offsets some of the energy cost savings. The NHTSA estimates that higher vehicle costs would reduce the consumer benefit of the MY2012–25 standards by 30 to 40 percent (NHTSA 2010), but that still leaves a net consumer savings larger than increased oil supply alone will deliver.

Equally important, vehicle efficiency helps safeguard the US economy from international energy supply disruptions in ways that increased domestic supply does not. As discussed in chapter 4, even if the United States becomes a net oil exporter in the years ahead, US pump prices will still follow international oil price movements. If there is a major global oil market disruption, US drivers will still feel the effect when they fill up. That more of the oil going into drivers' tanks was produced at home helps offset some of the macroeconomic effect of a price spike. Domestic oil producers will make more money and their shareholders may receive a greater dividend. But this does not help with the most important economic costs of an oil price spike: reduced consumer spending and auto industry dislocations as Americans' vehicle preferences change.

This is where fuel economy standards come in. The loss of consumer revenue during an oil price spike is significantly mitigated if Americans are driving more efficient vehicles. Current CAFE standards double the efficiency of new vehicles sold in the United States. It takes roughly seven years for the country's vehicle fleet to turn over; the fuel economy of the average car in the United States is affected by the rate of new car sales. But we estimate that by 2035 the US light-duty vehicle stock will be 67 percent more efficient than it is today. Standards help ensure that vehicle efficiency improvements continue if oil prices fall, protecting against future auto industry dislocations. When oil prices fell in the 1980s and progress on fuel economy standards stopped, so did vehicle efficiency improvements. That left the auto sector, and the economy as a whole, vulnerable when oil prices started rising again in 2002–03. The MY2012–25 standards allow the country to benefit from a potential drop in oil prices thanks to increased unconventional supply while safeguarding the economy from future price spikes.

Fuel Switching

Oil is not the only transportation fuel booming in the United States. Between 2005 and 2012, US biofuel production grew by nearly 700,000 bbl/d, which has affected US oil demand significantly. High oil prices and federal tax credits have driven the increase in biofuel output and corn-based ethanol, as the most commercially mature US biofuel technology—it has accounted for the vast majority of production.

Table 5.1   Renewable fuel standard volumetric requirements, 2006–22
(billions of gallons)

| Year | Conventional | Total | Advanced | | | | Total |
| | | | Cellulosic ethanol | | Biodiesel | | |
			Initial target	Actual mandate	Initial target	Actual mandate	
2006	4.0	n.a.	n.a.	n.a.	n.a.	n.a.	4.00
2007	7.7	n.a.	n.a.	n.a.	n.a.	n.a.	7.70
2008	9.0	n.a.	n.a.	n.a.	n.a.	n.a.	9.00
2009	10.5	0.60	n.a.	n.a.	0.50	0.50	11.10
2010	12.0	0.95	0.10	n.a.	0.65	0.65	12.95
2011	12.6	1.35	0.25	0.00660	0.80	0.80	13.95
2012	13.2	2.00	0.50	0.00865	1.00	1.00	15.20
2013	13.8	2.75	1.00		tbd	1.28	16.55
2014	14.5	3.75	1.75		tbd		18.15
2015	15.0	5.50	3.00		tbd		20.50
2016	15.0	7.25	4.25		tbd		22.25
2017	15.0	9.00	5.50		tbd		24.00
2018	15.0	11.00	7.00		tbd		26.00
2019	15.0	13.00	8.50		tbd		28.00
2020	15.0	15.00	10.50		tbd		30.00
2021	15.0	18.00	13.50		tbd		33.00
2022	15.0	21.00	16.00		tbd		36.00

n.a. = not available; tbd = to be determined

Sources: EPA (2010, 2011b, 2012a, 2012b).

The outlook for biofuels, however, is not as bright as for crude oil supply, at least for the next decade. Ethanol production fell during 2012 relative to 2011 levels as rising corn prices, falling oil prices, and the elimination of a key federal tax incentive squeezed producer profit margins. EISA revised a renewable fuels standard (RFS) enacted through previous legislation to require 36 billion gallons (2.3 million bbl/d) of biofuel supply in the United States by 2022 (table 5.1). That target is significantly higher than the roughly 1 million bbl/d of domestic biofuel output today, but only 15 billion gallons (980,000 bbl/d) can come from corn ethanol. The other 21 billion gallons must come from "advanced biofuels," 16 billion gallons of which must be cellulosic ethanol. To date, cellulosic ethanol production growth has been extremely slow, forcing the EPA to waive the RFS mandate each year. For 2012 only 8.65 million gallons of cellulosic ethanol are required, compared with the 500 million gallons called for in EISA. The most promising source of supply of other advanced biofuels has been imported Brazilian ethanol made from sugarcane. The EIA anticipates less than 20 billion gallons of US biofuel production by 2022, far short of the RFS target (EIA 2013e).

If the biofuel industry can deliver breakthrough advances in cellulosic ethanol, biodiesel, or other advanced biofuels in the years ahead, the United

States could become a net oil exporter as well as a net energy exporter overall by 2030. That would further improve the country's terms of trade and could reduce the price of transportation fuels in the United States and around the world. The overall economic effect on a barrel-for-barrel basis would be similar to increased domestic crude oil supply, rather than other oil demand–reducing measures such as vehicle efficiency improvements. As biofuel prices track oil product prices very closely, increased supply does not, in and of itself, safeguard the US economy from future oil price spikes.

Other types of fuel switching in the transportation sector, however, could have a more protective effect. Electricity prices have little correlation with oil prices and natural gas prices are becoming increasingly uncorrelated thanks to the domestic shale gas boom. Deployment of electric and natural gas vehicles has been quite limited to date, and had almost no effect on overall US oil demand. But significant growth in the years ahead would further reduce oil demand and the vulnerability of the US economy to oil price spikes.

Fuel switching outside the transportation sector has accelerated the decline in US oil demand and oil imports. Oil and natural gas are both used as a feedstock in petrochemical production. In the production of many products, such as ethylene and its downstream derivatives, they are also substitutes. Ethylene crackers use either ethane, a natural gas liquid (NGL) produced alongside dry natural gas, or naphtha, a petroleum product refined from crude oil. With the shale gas boom pushing down domestic natural gas and NGL prices, the petrochemical industry is substituting ethane for naphtha wherever possible, leading to a significant decline in overall US naphtha demand. In addition to lowering US oil imports, this switch has made US petrochemical producers more competitive relative to their naphtha-dependent peers in Europe and Asia, discussed in depth in the next chapter.

Summing Up

As this book focuses on the economic implications of the recent increase in US oil and gas supply, we did not conduct the same macroeconomic analysis on the changes in oil demand discussed above. But increased oil and gas supply complements improved efficiency and fuel switching; it does not replace the need for it. Higher oil and gas supply lowers energy prices, improves US terms of trade, and provides some much-needed economic stimulus. But it alone does not protect the economy from global price volatility. Efficiency improvements that reduce energy's importance in economic output, along with the development of alternative sources of energy that increase options for substitution, remain vital elements of a smart energy strategy, particularly given the uncertainty regarding the US oil and gas supply in the future.

6

Regional and Sectoral Consequences

The economic benefits of the US oil and gas renaissance described in chapter 4 will not be spread evenly across the country. Some states will be helped far more than others thanks to their geology. However, increased oil and gas production in these states will boost economic activity more broadly by creating demand for goods and services produced in other parts of the country. Some industries will become more competitive internationally due to lower US energy costs while others will see competitiveness erode due to higher-cost labor and capital or a stronger US dollar. Even the economic gains from lower household energy expenditures—the most important factor at the national level—vary considerably from region to region.

Rise of the American Petrostate

In 2010 the media began noticing that, in a nation struggling to emerge from recession, one state appeared to be thriving. Tucked away in the upper Great Plains, the 700,000 residents of North Dakota seemed immune to the economic malaise affecting the rest of the country. At its worst, the unemployment rate in the state had reached a mere 4.2 percent, compared with a nationwide high of 10 percent (figure 6.1). News reports of families relocating to North Dakota in search of work, only to find a housing shortage once they arrived, began appearing in the national press.[1] The tight oil boom discussed in chapter 3 was soaking up just about all the spare labor North Dakota had to offer and drawing engineers and mudloggers, as well as truckers, construction, and food

1. Monica Davey, "A State with Plenty of Jobs but Few Places to Live," *New York Times*, April 20, 2010, www.nytimes.com/2010/04/21/us/21ndakota.html (accessed on September 8, 2013).

Figure 6.1 Unemployment rates in North and South Dakota, 1995–2012

percent

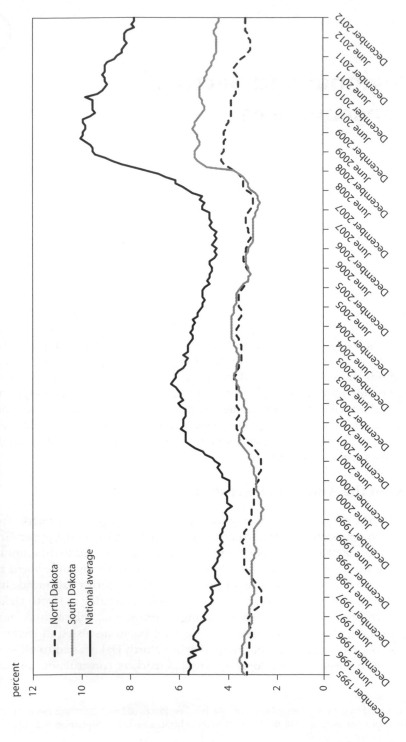

Source: BLS (2013a).

service workers, from across the country—just as petrostates in the Middle East import skilled workers from Texas and construction workers from Bangladesh and Pakistan.

North Dakota has become a poster child for those hoping that a rebound in US oil and gas supply will save the US economy.[2] Presidential candidate Mitt Romney gave an energy policy speech there in March 2012[3] and the state's junior senator, John Hoeven, was chosen as the spokesman for congressional Republicans' energy legislation later that year. In 2012 North Dakota became the first state in the country to return to its precrisis unemployment levels, an enviably low 3 percent.

The North Dakota experience, however, is not replicable at a national level. First, unemployment there is structurally lower than it is in other states. North Dakota averaged 3.2 percent unemployment in the decade before the crisis, a period in which oil production was flat, at roughly 100,000 barrels per day (bbl/d). South Dakota's unemployment rate was about the same despite having no meaningful oil industry (figure 6.1). That said, following the crisis, the spike in unemployment was smaller and shorter in North Dakota than in its southern neighbor, thanks primarily to the exponential growth of the Bakken oil supply.

For other major oil- and gas-producing states, however, the picture is more mixed. Figure 6.2 shows the change in unemployment rate between 2007 and 2012. States with more than 250,000 barrels of oil equivalent (boe) per day of combined oil and gas production in 2012 are shown in dark gray. A number of these states—Alaska, Oklahoma, Arkansas, Kansas, and Texas—are doing considerably better than the national average. But others—Utah, Wyoming, Colorado, New Mexico, and California—are not.

Part of the disparity is explained by the size of the state. As a number of analysts have pointed out, a drilling boom cannot have the same effect in Pennsylvania (population 13 million) as in North Dakota (population 700,000) even though both states produced about the same amount of oil and gas on a boe basis in 2012.[4] Oil and gas production accounts for 5.42 percent of total employment in North Dakota. In Pennsylvania it accounts for less than 0.5

2. Ed Whitfield, Opening Statement of the Honorable Ed Whitfield—Hearing on The American Energy Initiative: A Focus on the Outlook for Achieving North American Energy Independence Within the Decade, 2012, http://energycommerce.house.gov/sites/republicans.energycommerce.house.gov/files/Hearings/EP/20120913/HHRG-112-IF03-MState-W000413-20120913.pdf (accessed on September 8, 2013). See also Stephen Moore, "What North Dakota Could Teach California," Wall Street Journal, March 11, 2012.

3. Emily Friedman, "Romney Delivers Counter Argument to Obama's Energy Speech," ABC News, March 1, 2012, http://abcnews.go.com/blogs/politics/2012/03/romney-delivers-counter-argument-to-obamas-energy-speech (accessed on September 8, 2013).

4. Michael A. Levi, "Did Natural Gas Save the Pennsylvania Economy?" Council on Foreign Relations, March 14, 2012, http://blogs.cfr.org/levi/2012/03/14/did-natural-gas-save-the-pennsylvania-economy (accessed on September 8, 2013).

Figure 6.2 Change in unemployment rates, by state, 2007–12

percent

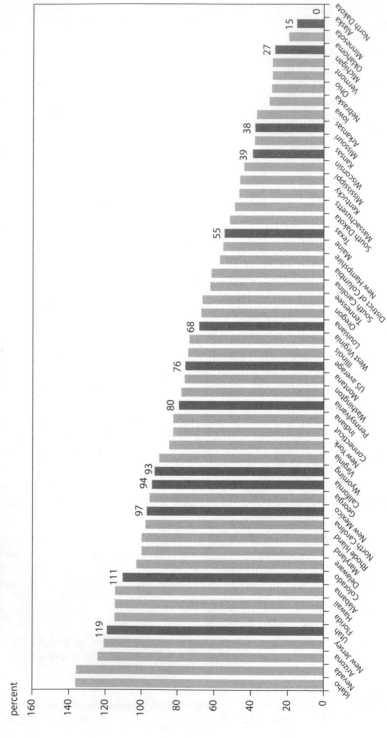

Source: BLS (2013a).

percent (table 6.1). Another factor is the rate of growth in the state's production. The front end of the oil and gas production cycle—exploration, drilling, and well completion—is the most labor intensive. Once the wells are producing, the number of workers required to keep things running drops off. This is less true for shale gas and tight oil plays, where wells have steep decline rates and operators must keep fracking new wells, or refracking existing wells, to maintain production. That said, states where production is growing should see larger employment effects than similar states where production is relatively flat. This is clear when comparing North Dakota, where production is growing, with Wyoming, where production is relatively flat. Wyoming produced 1,221,000 boe/d of oil and gas in 2012, compared with 736,000 boe/d for North Dakota. Yet there were more than 22,000 oil and gas employees in North Dakota, compared with fewer than 18,000 in Wyoming. Oil's and gas's share of statewide employment in North Dakota grew from 1 to 5.4 percent between 2007 and 2012, accounting for 27 percent of total employment growth in the state during that period. In Wyoming, oil and gas declined as a share of total employment (table 6.1 and figure 6.3). The balance between oil and gas in a state's production portfolio also shapes local economic effects, given the current price disparity between the two fuels. Even in the most energy-rich states, oil and gas production is only one of many factors driving employment and economic growth.

Figure 6.3 combines some of the variables above to provide a snapshot of America's emerging petrostates. The x-axis is the share of state employment in the oil and gas industry in the first to third quarters of 2012, the most recent data available at time of publication. The y-axis is the change in this share between the first and third quarters of 2007 and the first and third quarters of 2012. The circle size represents total oil and gas employment in the state. Dark grey circles are states where at least one-third of the output, in boe terms, is crude oil. Light grey circles are states where more than two-thirds is natural gas. Medium grey circles are those with less than 250,000 boe per day of oil and gas production in 2012, but where oil and gas as a share of state employment are greater than 0.1 percent and rising. Not surprisingly North Dakota has the highest growth in oil and gas employment as a share of total employment and the second-highest share of oil and gas employment in 2012. Texas has the largest number of oil and gas employees, but the state's 25 million residents dilute those numbers. Likewise, in Pennsylvania the economic benefits of the oil and gas boom are reduced because most of the state's output is natural gas. Stagnant or declining production in Wyoming in recent years partly explains why unemployment rates have not fallen as fast as similarly sized North Dakota, but unemployment rates in Kansas and Mississippi have declined considerably faster than the national average despite very little growth in oil and gas employment, suggesting other factors play a more important role.

In the future, Rocky Mountain and Gulf Coast states are likely to see the most direct economic benefit from growth in US oil and gas supply. In the Rockies, high-caliber shale gas, tight oil, and oil shale resources combined with low population density create a significant per capita economic upside. Gulf Coast states stand to benefit from a combination of onshore unconventional

Table 6.1   Oil and gas employment, by state, 2007 and 2012

State	2007Q1–Q3		2012Q1–Q3		2012 versus 2007	
	Employees	Percent share of total	Employees	Percent share of total	Employees	Percent change in share of total
Alabama	1,851	0.10	1,741	0.10	−110	0.00
Alaska	11,738	3.75	13,738	4.17	2,000	0.42
Arizona	307	0.01	639	0.03	332	0.01
Arkansas	4,592	0.39	6,815	0.60	2,222	0.20
California	18,497	0.12	22,776	0.15	4,279	0.03
Colorado	19,061	0.83	24,879	1.10	5,817	0.27
Connecticut	0	0.00	40	0.00	40	0.00
Delaware	0	0.00	0	0.00	0	0.00
District of Columbia	0	0.00	0	0.00	0	0.00
Florida	599	0.01	668	0.01	69	0.00
Georgia	0	0.00	0	0.00	0	0.00
Hawaii	0	0.00	0	0.00	0	0.00
Idaho	223	0.03	433	0.07	209	0.04
Illinois	2,421	0.04	3,207	0.06	787	0.02
Indiana	323	0.01	656	0.02	334	0.01
Iowa	11	0.00	23	0.00	12	0.00
Kansas	8,012	0.59	8,576	0.65	564	0.06
Kentucky	3,846	0.21	3,772	0.22	−74	0.00
Louisiana	46,694	2.51	51,437	2.76	4,743	0.25
Maine	0	0.00	0	0.00	0	0.00
Maryland	434	0.02	0	0.00	−434	−0.02
Massachusetts	0	0.00	87	0.00	87	0.00
Michigan	2,382	0.06	2,714	0.07	331	0.01
Minnesota	0	0.00	246	0.01	246	0.01
Mississippi	5,332	0.47	5,642	0.52	311	0.05
Missouri	567	0.02	312	0.01	−255	−0.01
Montana	3,001	0.69	3,772	0.88	771	0.19
Nebraska	244	0.03	285	0.03	41	0.00
Nevada	1,207	0.09	2,435	0.22	1,228	0.12
New Hampshire	0	0.00	88	0.01	88	0.01
New Jersey	0	0.00	265	0.01	265	0.01
New Mexico	15,304	1.87	18,680	2.39	3,375	0.52
New York	866	0.01	1,176	0.01	311	0.00
North Carolina	0	0.00	312	0.01	312	0.01
North Dakota	3,454	1.02	22,093	5.42	18,639	4.40
Ohio	5,447	0.10	6,333	0.13	886	0.02
Oklahoma	43,446	2.85	55,758	3.65	12,312	0.80
Oregon	52	0.00	0	0.00	−52	0.00
Pennsylvania	6,804	0.12	22,518	0.40	15,715	0.28
Rhode Island	0	0.00	0	0.00	0	0.00
South Carolina	49	0.00	0	0.00	−49	0.00
South Dakota	83	0.02	74	0.02	−9	0.00
Tennessee	608	0.02	412	0.02	−196	−0.01
Texas	192,915	1.90	257,112	2.41	64,197	0.52

(table continues next page)

Table 6.1   Oil and gas employment, by state, 2007 and 2012 *(continued)*

State	2007Q1–Q3 Employees	2007Q1–Q3 Percent share of total	2012Q1–Q3 Employees	2012Q1–Q3 Percent share of total	2012 versus 2007 Employees	2012 versus 2007 Percent change in share of total
Utah	6,145	0.51	7,398	0.61	1,253	0.11
Vermont	0	0.00	0	0.00	0	0.00
Virginia	2,061	0.06	1,786	0.05	–274	–0.01
Washington	198	0.01	0	0.00	–198	–0.01
West Virginia	7,892	1.12	9,185	1.29	1,293	0.17
Wisconsin	0	0.00	0	0.00	0	0.00
Wyoming	18,106	6.54	17,807	6.40	–298	–0.15
US total	435,832	0.32	577,381	0.44	141,549	0.12

Note: Employment in oil and gas extraction and support activities, the first and third quarters of 2007 and the first and third quarters of 2012.

Source: BLS (2013b).

Figure 6.3   American petrostates

change in oil and gas employment as a share of total, 2012Q1–Q3 versus 2007Q1–Q3 (percent)

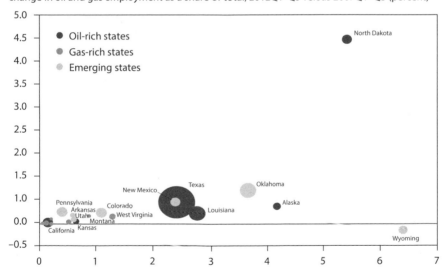

oil and gas employment as a share of total, 2012Q1–Q3 (percent)

Note: Circle size denotes total oil and gas employment in 2012Q1–Q3.

Sources: EIA (2013a, 2013b); BLS (2013b).

oil and gas development, growth in offshore exploration, and production in the Gulf of Mexico as well as oil and gas development in other parts of the country thanks to the large share of the energy industry headquartered in Houston. The investment required to bring this production online will provide the most economic benefit by creating demand for manufacturing, construction, and service sector activity (indirect effects). Except at filling stations, where average wages are among the worst in the country, oil and gas industry jobs also pay better than average everywhere along the value chain. Overall this means additional induced economic benefits in Rocky Mountain and Gulf Coast states when oil and gas workers spend their paychecks.

As discussed in chapter 4, the indirect and induced effects of an increase in oil and gas investment matter most over the next few years, when the economy is still returning to full employment. In the long run, oil and gas will compete with other sectors for labor and investment capital, pushing up prices. This is already occurring in North Dakota, where the state economy is back to precrisis employment levels. Since the crisis, North Dakota has seen some of the most impressive wage growth in the country. Hourly private sector wages rose 5.6 percent per year on average between 2009 and 2011, the third-fastest increase in the country after Oklahoma and the District of Columbia (BLS 2013a). But inflation, as measured by the Bureau of Economic Analysis GDP deflator, rose even faster—8.3 percent per year between 2009 and 2011 (BEA 2013). North Dakotans profit from the oil and gas boom beyond their paychecks—through, for example, royalty payments to landowners—but inflation is already taking a big bite out of the net benefit they receive.

Other regions outside the Rockies and the Gulf Coast will benefit from the oil and gas boom as well. Midwest and New England states could see meaningful production growth from the Utica and Marcellus shales, but given higher population density, it is unlikely to have much of a direct effect on overall economic activity or employment in either region. These regions are, however, benefiting in other ways: through increased demand for the manufactured goods used in the oil and gas industry, lower energy bills for households and businesses, and potentially improved international competitiveness due to lower energy costs.

A Manufacturing Renaissance?

Shortly after the boom in US oil and gas production gained national attention, commentators began speculating it could lead to a rebirth of US manufacturing (PwC 2011, Verleger 2012).[5] Increased drilling activity has boosted demand for a range of manufactured goods, from the steel pipe used in the production process itself to the cement and glass required to build housing for

---

5. See also David Ignatius, "An Economic Boom Ahead?" *Washington Post*, May 4, 2012, www.washingtonpost.com/opinions/an-economic-boom-ahead/2012/05/04/gIQAbj5K2T_story.html (accessed on September 8, 2013).

oil and gas workers. Anecdotal reports suggested this new demand has led to new factories opening in the Midwest, after years of industrial decay.[6]

As discussed in chapter 4, the increase in employment and industrial output in the oil and gas industry itself is known in economic parlance as a direct effect. This creates demand for intermediate goods and services (indirect effects) and broader economic and employment activity when employees in the oil and gas or supporting industries spend their paychecks (induced effects). A 2012 IHS Cambridge Energy Research Associates (CERA) report assessed the direct, indirect, and induced effects of all unconventional oil and gas production using the impact analysis for planning (IMPLAN) input-output model of the US economy (also used in the Wood Mackenzie, Mckinsey, and American Chemistry Council studies discussed in chapter 4).[7] The report estimates that by 2035, unconventional oil and gas production will support 725,379 jobs directly, 1,074,155 indirectly, and another 1,700,144 through induced effects. However, this does not mean that overall US employment will grow by 3.5 million jobs. Many will come at the expense of employment in other sectors, and even other parts of the oil and gas sector, such as deepwater, where IHS CERA projects a production decline. Accounting for general equilibrium effects, we estimate in chapter 4 that the oil and gas boom will increase net US employment by up to 1.1 million jobs in 2035 (optimistic scenario). But IHS CERA's approach is valuable in examining which industries stand to gain the most from an increase in oil and gas investment.

Using IHS CERA's estimates of the investment requirements of new oil and gas production and the sectoral distribution of that investment demand, we analyzed the effect of a $95 billion increase in annual oil and gas investment—the difference between our optimistic and pre-shale cases—on industrial output and employment using the IMPLAN model, capturing direct, indirect, and induced effects. Combining these three effects, the mining sector sees the largest gains, with a 10 percent increase in output and an 11 percent increase in employment relative to 2010 levels (table 6.2). The utilities sector also sees a meaningful increase, of roughly 2 percent, in output, while service sector gains are largely less than 1 percent.

Some segments of the manufacturing sector stand to benefit greatly from the increase in demand created by an oil and gas investment boom. Table 6.3 lists the top 20 manufacturing beneficiaries by absolute increase in employment due to an additional $95 billion in annual oil and gas investment. Cutting tool and machine tool accessory manufacturing adds 48,300 jobs in our analysis, while oil and gas machinery manufacturing adds 20,500 jobs. The steel industry

6. Keith Schneider, "As Demand Rises, Ohio's Steel Mills Shake Off the Rust and Expand," *New York Times*, April 24, 2012, www.nytimes.com/2012/04/25/business/energy-environment/ohio-steel-mills-expand-to-meet-demand-in-energy-and-auto-industries.html (accessed on September 8, 2013).

7. For information on the IMPLAN model, see http://implan.com (accessed on September 8, 2013).

Table 6.2 Impact of increased oil and gas investment, by sector

Sector	Employment			Output		
	2010 levels (thousands)	Optimistic versus pre-shale		2010 levels (billions of 2010 US dollars)	Optimistic versus pre-shale	
		Thousands	Percent change from 2010		Billions of 2010 US dollars	Percent change from 2010
Agriculture and forestry	3,428	17.1	0.50	383	2.0	0.51
Mining	1,351	153.6	11.37	381	39.3	10.30
Utilities	581	23.1	3.98	390	8.8	2.27
Construction	8,998	92.6	1.03	1,210	13.4	1.11
Manufacturing	11,759	256.3	2.18	5,623	101.5	1.81
Wholesale trade	5,852	44.0	0.75	1,008	7.6	0.75
Retail trade	17,454	106.4	0.61	1,137	6.9	0.61
Transportation and warehousing	5,351	60.1	1.12	689	7.7	1.12
Information	3,164	21.1	0.67	1,096	7.1	0.65
Finance	10,856	91.3	0.84	2,334	19.7	0.84
Real estate	6,666	44.4	0.67	2,176	13.9	0.64
Professional services	12,865	114.4	0.89	1,868	17.4	0.93
Company management	11,910	108.2	0.91	991	9.9	1.00
Education and social services	22,567	130.9	0.58	1,991	11.5	0.58
Arts and entertainment	3,688	25.0	0.68	222	1.5	0.67
Hotels and restaurants	11,978	82.9	0.69	721	5.1	0.70
Other services	9,812	123.8	1.26	679	5.4	0.79
Government	1,893	14.0	0.74	357	2.7	0.75

Note: Increase in annual output and employment resulting from the average difference in oil and gas investment between the pre-shale and optimistic scenarios between 2013 and 2035, compared with 2010 output levels.

Source: Authors' calculations.

Table 6.3 Top 20 manufacturing beneficiaries, by absolute increase in employment

Industry	2010 levels (thousands)	Optimistic versus pre-shale Thousands	Optimistic versus pre-shale Percent change from 2010	2010 levels (billions of 2010 US dollars)	Optimistic versus pre-shale Billions of 2010 US dollars	Optimistic versus pre-shale Percent change from 2010
		Employment			**Output**	
Cutting tool and machine tool accessory manufacturing	21.5	48.3	225.0	3.0	7.6	249.3
Mining and oil and gas field machinery manufacturing	70.6	20.5	29.1	34.2	10.9	31.9
Steel product manufacturing from purchased steel	52.6	18.8	35.7	23.4	9.1	38.9
Air and gas compressor manufacturing	19.1	13.9	73.1	9.6	7.7	80.8
Fabricated pipe and pipe fitting manufacturing	28.0	10.6	37.9	7.3	3.0	41.5
Pump and pumping equipment manufacturing	28.7	10.6	36.7	11.2	4.5	40.6
Machine shops	246.3	8.1	3.3	35.3	1.2	3.3
Metal tank (heavy gauge) manufacturing	27.9	7.8	28.1	6.2	1.9	31.1
Iron and steel mills and ferroalloy manufacturing	86.5	6.0	6.9	60.0	4.2	6.9
All other basic inorganic chemical manufacturing	30.4	5.2	17.1	22.8	4.3	18.9
Ferrous metal foundries	65.1	4.4	6.7	15.1	1.0	6.7
Industrial gas manufacturing	17.6	4.0	22.7	18.0	4.5	24.9
Other electronic component manufacturing	58.7	4.0	6.8	12.5	0.9	7.4
Coating, engraving, heat-treating, and allied activities	124.2	3.5	2.8	23.4	0.7	2.8
Printing	496.1	3.2	0.6	77.0	0.5	0.6
Plate work and fabricated structural product manufacturing	149.8	3.1	2.1	36.9	0.8	2.1
Industrial process variable instruments manufacturing	53.2	3.1	5.8	15.3	0.9	6.1
Other plastic products manufacturing	271.8	2.9	1.1	63.8	0.7	1.1
Motor vehicle parts manufacturing	413.4	2.7	0.7	158.3	1.0	0.7
Ornamental and architectural metal products manufacturing	176.9	2.4	1.3	33.9	0.5	1.3

Note: Increase in annual output and employment resulting from the average difference in oil and gas investment between the pre-shale and optimistic scenarios between 2013 and 2035, compared with 2010 output levels.

Source: Authors' calculations using the National Energy Modeling System and data from the Minnesota IMPLAN Group and IHS CERA (2012).

does well also, with seven steel production subcategories making the top 20 list. As a percent increase, nine manufacturing industries see double-digit gains in output and employment (table 6.4), three of which are steel subcategories (fabricated pipes and fittings, steel product manufacturing from purchased steel, and metal tanks). Cement, gasket, spring, and wire manufacturing also do pretty well.

The above industries, however, account for a fairly small share of the manufacturing sector as a whole. Industries that could see a greater than 10 percent increase in demand thanks to higher oil and gas investment account for only 2.5 percent of total manufacturing employment (figure 6.4). Industries that could see a 5 to 10 percent increase in demand account for another 3.1 percent. But for 94.3 percent of the manufacturing sector, the increase in employment would be less than 5 percent, and less than 1 percent for 73 percent of the sector. If the US oil and gas boom creates a true manufacturing renaissance, it will have to come from increased international competitiveness thanks to lower energy costs.

Energy, like labor and capital, is a cost of production for most businesses. By lowering natural gas and electricity prices, the shale boom has already reduced costs for some manufacturing industries and made them more internationally competitive. In 2005 the average price industrial consumers paid for natural gas in the United States was higher than in China, on par with Europe, and only 20 percent lower than Japan. By 2011 US industrial consumers were paying less than half as much as their counterparts in Europe and China, and a quarter as much as industrial consumers in Japan. Electricity prices have fallen in the United States as well, while they have increased in most other parts of the world.

The decrease in relative energy costs matters a lot for some industries and hardly at all for others. Energy costs as a share of overall product value range from 50 to 60 percent for fertilizer manufacturing to less than 0.5 percent for automobile and airplane manufacturing. To assess the implications of a US oil and gas renaissance on manufacturing competitiveness, we analyzed how the difference in energy prices between our pre-shale and optimistic scenarios changes each industry's production costs.[8] As table 6.5 shows, a few industries could see double-digit reductions in overall production costs: petrochemicals, fertilizer, plastic materials, carbon black, and other basic organic chemicals.

US petrochemical producers rely on ethane, a natural gas liquid (NGL), as their primary feedstock in producing ethylene, compared with competitors in Europe and Asia that rely on the crude oil derivative naphtha. As US NGL

---

8. We take energy consumption data from the Manufacturing Energy Consumption Survey (EIA 2013f) and shipment value data from the American Manufacturing Survey (Census Bureau 2012) for 2010, the latest year for which data are available from both. We then calculate energy costs as a share of shipment value using price projections from our pre-shale and optimistic scenarios, updating shipment value to reflect the change in energy costs relative to 2010 levels. This assumes no change in technical efficiency or fuel substitution at different energy price levels and thus should be treated as a rough estimate. Petroleum refining and other energy transformation businesses classified as manufacturing are excluded.

Table 6.4 Top 20 manufacturing beneficiaries, by percent change in employment and output

Industry	Employment 2010 levels (thousands)	Employment Optimistic versus pre-shale Thousands	Employment Optimistic versus pre-shale Percent change from 2010	Output 2010 levels (billions of 2010 US dollars)	Output Optimistic versus pre-shale Billions of 2010 US dollars	Output Optimistic versus pre-shale Percent change from 2010
Cutting tool and machine tool accessory manufacturing	21.5	48.3	225.0	3.0	7.6	249.3
Air and gas compressor manufacturing	19.1	13.9	73.1	9.6	7.7	80.8
Fabricated pipe and pipe fitting manufacturing	28.0	10.6	37.9	7.3	3.0	41.5
Pump and pumping equipment manufacturing	28.7	10.6	36.7	11.2	4.5	40.6
Steel product manufacturing from purchased steel	52.6	18.8	35.7	23.4	9.1	38.9
Mining and oil and gas field machinery manufacturing	70.6	20.5	29.1	34.2	10.9	31.9
Metal tank (heavy gauge) manufacturing	27.9	7.8	28.1	6.2	1.9	31.1
Industrial gas manufacturing	17.6	4.0	22.7	18.0	4.5	24.9
All other basic inorganic chemical manufacturing	30.4	5.2	17.1	22.8	4.3	18.9
Cement manufacturing	13.9	1.1	8.1	5.5	0.5	8.7
Ground or treated mineral and earth manufacturing	6.4	0.5	7.3	4.1	0.3	7.3
Iron and steel mills and ferroalloy manufacturing	86.5	6.0	6.9	60.0	4.2	6.9
Other electronic component manufacturing	58.7	4.0	6.8	12.5	0.9	7.4
Ferrous metal foundries	65.1	4.4	6.7	15.1	1.0	6.7
Gasket, packing, and sealing device manufacturing	31.2	1.9	6.0	5.8	0.4	6.0
Industrial process variable instruments manufacturing	53.2	3.1	5.8	15.3	0.9	6.1
Miscellaneous nonmetallic mineral products manufacturing	11.1	0.6	5.7	3.8	0.2	5.7
Spring and wire product manufacturing	42.2	2.3	5.5	9.2	0.5	5.5
All other forging, stamping, and sintering	35.6	1.7	4.7	9.7	0.5	4.7
Nonferrous metal (except copper and aluminum) rolling, drawing, extruding, and alloying	22.2	1.0	4.5	13.9	0.6	4.5

Note: Increase in annual output and employment resulting from the average difference in oil and gas investment between the pre-shale and optimistic scenarios between 2013 and 2035, compared with 2010 output levels.

Source: Authors' calculations using the National Energy Modeling System and data from the Minnesota IMPLAN Group and IHS CERA (2012).

Figure 6.4   Distribution of US manufacturing by positive exposure to increased oil and gas investment, 2010

percent share of manufacturing employment

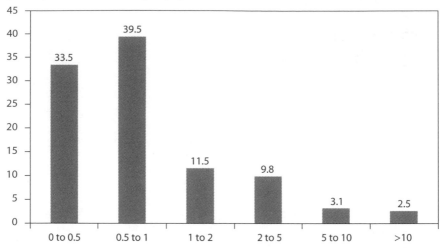

percent increase in employment from higher oil and gas investment

Source: Authors' calculations.

supply has risen alongside dry natural gas production, the price of ethane and other NGLs has fallen. Ethane prices traditionally follow naphtha prices, and thus crude oil prices, as they are substitutes in petrochemical production. The recent surge in natural gas production has broken this link and ethane prices have fallen sharply (figure 6.5). As a result, US ethylene producers have become highly competitive internationally and seen strong profit growth (Koort, Maguire, and Gupta 2012; Juvekar et al. 2012). If ethane prices maintain their current discount relative to crude oil prices, US petrochemical operating costs will be up to 18 percent lower on average in the optimistic scenario than in the pre-shale scenario between 2013 and 2035 (table 6.5).

Analysts have grown more confident of the durability of the current shale gas boom, and as a result, the US chemical industry is considering investment in an additional 8 million to 10 million tons of ethylene capacity in the years ahead. That would expand US ethylene capacity by 30 to 38 percent (International E Chem 2012, Collins et al. 2012, Morse et al. 2012). Many of these projects are de-bottlenecking operations or brownfield expansions, but several greenfield projects have been announced as well. It is unlikely that all of these plants will be built, and several already have been delayed (Juvekar and Khan 2012, Collins et al. 2012). But the US petrochemical industry is well positioned to expand thanks to the domestic oil and gas boom. Fertilizer production, which relies on natural gas as a primary feedstock, is also expanding, as is output of other chemical products.

Table 6.5   Industrial implications of growing oil and gas supply

Industry	Number of employees, 2011	Potential cost savings[a] (percent change in energy expenditures/ shipment value)	Net export orientation (percent)
Food	1,358,996	0.6	2.1
Grain and oilseed milling	50,499	1.0	8.8
Sugar manufacturing	13,222	1.8	0.7
Fruit and vegetable preserving and specialty foods	160,869	0.8	2.9
Dairy products	130,791	0.4	−1.3
Animal slaughtering and processing	474,400	0.5	4.1
Beverage and tobacco products	139,966	0.2	−1.6
Textile mills	103,454	1.1	12.3
Textile product mills	106,836	0.3	−2.1
Apparel	95,176	0.2	9.6
Leather and allied products	26,953	0.1	34.9
Wood products	324,870	0.6	−2.9
Paper	346,439	1.3	6.1
Pulp mills	6,889	1.4	108.7
Paper mills	65,740	1.9	4.4
Paperboard mills	34,902	2.2	−7.9
Printing and related support	456,897	0.4	0.3
Petroleum and coal products	98,249	2.1	−27.2
Chemicals	693,566	6.9	14.5
Petrochemicals	8,797	17.6	−12.2
Industrial gases	9,671	7.2	1.0
Alkalies and chlorine	5,959	2.3	19.1
Carbon black	1,672	14.0	10.6
Other basic inorganic chemicals	29,674	2.6	27.6
Other basic organic chemicals	78,463	12.2	26.1
Plastic materials and resins	57,589	17.8	20.4
Synthetic rubber	9,401	2.0	41.3
Artificial and synthetic fibers	13,228	1.9	6.5
Nitrogenous fertilizers	4,338	13.4	−4.0
Phosphatic fertilizers	5,892	0.2	30.1
Pharmaceuticals and medicines	221,283	0.2	12.3
Plastics and rubber products	674,690	0.6	2.0
Nonmetallic mineral products	333,868	1.9	4.8
Flat glass	7,840	6.6	43.9
Other pressed and blown glass and glassware	16,315	3.3	33.2
Glass containers	13,636	4.1	3.3
Glass products from purchased glass	38,551	0.5	1.6
Cements	12,360	4.0	−0.9
Lime	4,373	2.8	−0.3
Gypsum	7,495	4.9	5.5
Mineral wool	15,321	2.6	9.5

(table continues next page)

Table 6.5   Industrial implications of growing oil and gas supply *(continued)*

Industry	Number of employees, 2011	Potential cost savings[a] (percent change in energy expenditures/ shipment value)	Net export orientation (percent)
Primary metals	373,911	1.6	9.6
Iron and steel mills and ferroalloy products	100,247	2.1	7.7
Steel products from purchased steel	40,291	0.7	–13.9
Alumina and aluminum	51,059	2.4	–4.3
Nonferrous metals except aluminum	56,935	0.8	29.5
Foundries	123,500	1.2	–6.6
Fabricated metal products	1,285,707	0.4	1.6
Machinery	964,668	0.2	27.4
Computer and electronic products	816,676	0.2	25.3
Electrical equipment, appliances, and components	328,446	0.3	16.6
Transportation equipment	1,235,431	0.2	10.7
Cars and light trucks	120,691	0.1	–3.2
Aerospace products and parts	401,961	0.2	28.0
Furniture and related products	319,869	0.3	–1.7
Miscellaneous	564,709	0.1	18.3

a. Assumes ethane prices converge to natural gas levels in the optimistic scenario and remain at crude oil parity in the pre-shale scenario.

Sources: Authors' calculations using the National Energy Modeling System; EIA (2013f); Census Bureau (2012); BEA (2013); Goldberg and Crockett (1998).

The direct effect of improved US chemical industry competitiveness on employment and output is relatively limited. Production of petrochemicals, nitrogen fertilizer, carbon black, plastic materials, and other basic organic chemicals employs roughly 150,000 people combined, which translates to 1.3 percent of US manufacturing employment. Even if these industries doubled their output in the years ahead, the direct labor market effect would be minimal. Potentially more significant is the investment associated with new chemical industry capacity. The American Chemistry Council estimates that a 25 percent increase in domestic ethane supply from unconventional gas development could prompt $16.2 billion in additional chemical industry investment, with the attendant indirect and induced economic effects. Spread over the 2013–20 period, this would add just under $2 billion a year, in 2005 chained dollars, to the $95 billion increased annual investment in oil and gas production in our optimistic scenario and further enhance the short- and medium-term economic benefit of the unconventional boom discussed in chapter 4.

Other parts of the chemicals industry do not benefit quite as much from the oil and gas boom as ethylene, fertilizer, plastic materials, and other organic chemicals. On average, energy costs as a share of shipment value in the sector fall by 6.9 percent (table 6.5). Outside chemicals, the industries that derive a

Figure 6.5 **Naphtha and ethane prices compared with crude oil and natural gas prices, 2001–12**

US dollars per million British thermal units

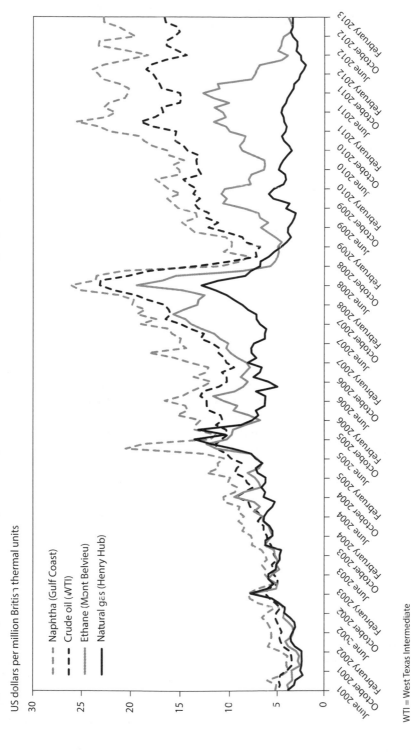

WTI = West Texas Intermediate

Source: Bloomberg.

Figure 6.6   Distribution of US manufacturing by potential cost reduction from lower energy prices

percent share of manufacturing employment, 2011

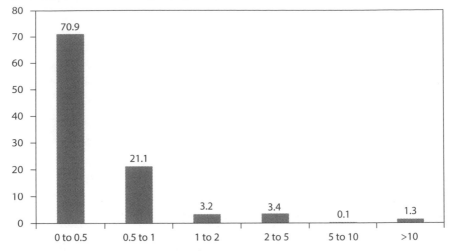

reduction in energy costs as a share of shipment value (percent)

Source: Authors' calculations.

meaningful production cost advantage from lower-cost domestic energy are limited in number. Industries that see more than a 2 percent reduction in energy costs as a share of shipment value as a result of the change in energy prices between our pre-shale and optimistic scenarios account for roughly 5 percent of total manufacturing employment (figure 6.6). These include nonmetallic mineral products, such as cement, glass, and lime, as well as some types of steel, aluminum, and paper production. Ninety-two percent of manufacturing employment is in industries for which the change in production costs is less than 1 percent. This includes most food and beverage production, fabricated metal products, machinery, computers and electronics, electronic equipment, furniture, automobiles, and airplanes.

For low domestic energy costs to translate into a sustained competitive advantage for those few industries that are experiencing a competitiveness boon today, energy prices will need to remain high in other parts of the world. While crude oil prices are meaningfully lower in our optimistic scenario than in the pre-shale case, they are lower for everyone. It is the natural gas market that is geographically disconnected, allowing for large differentials both in natural gas prices and electricity generated with natural gas. While the gap between US and Asian natural gas prices has reached historical highs, there is no guarantee it will stay there.

The gas-rich shale reservoirs driving North America's current production boom exist in other parts of the world as well. In 2011 the Energy Information

Administration (EIA) commissioned an assessment of technically recoverable shale gas resources in 32 countries. The United States ranked high on the list but not the highest: That honor went to China, with an estimated 1,275 trillion cubic feet (tcf) of shale gas resources. Later that year, China's Ministry of Land and Resources published its own estimate of 897 tcf, lower than the EIA's number but still higher than the US figure. The EIA report also found significant resources in Latin America, Africa, and Europe, some of which are already being developed.

It is unlikely that other countries will be able to immediately replicate the United States' recent shale gas experience. As discussed in chapter 4, it took more than a decade for George Mitchell's early experiments with hydraulic fracturing to lead to shale gas production volumes significant enough to lower prices. Much of the learning that occurred during that period is portable to other countries, but much of it is not. There are important geological differences among shale resources in various parts of the world. And there is a certain amount of time required to scale up operations and supply chains once the drilling techniques are mastered. There are also plenty of above-ground challenges, from environmental opposition in Europe to population resettlement in China. These will take time to sort out, but so long as the price of natural gas in Asia and Europe stays at its currently elevated levels, there will be a strong commercial incentive to do so.

US trade policy could also affect the current margin between US and international natural gas prices. The US government is evaluating a number of applications to export natural gas in the form of LNG, and has already approved several terminals. Gas-consuming industries are concerned that this could push domestic prices towards current European or Asian levels, thus eroding their newfound energy and feedstock cost advantage. Price convergence also could happen if US exports reduce the price of natural gas in other parts of the world. This would still erode the competitive advantage of energy-intensive US manufacturing, but it could have significant macroeconomic and environmental benefits as well. We analyze these questions in more depth in chapter 8.

Gains in energy-intensive manufacturing output and employment must also be scored against losses in industries vulnerable to the real effective exchange rate appreciation that is likely to occur—through either domestic inflation or nominal appreciation—thanks to a lower US energy trade deficit (see chapter 4). Linda Goldberg and Keith Crockett (1998) measure an industry's vulnerability to exchange rate appreciation by its "net export orientation." Net export orientation is "the share of an industry's total revenues that is derived from exports less the share of its total spending that is attributable to imported inputs." Industries with a positive net export orientation are harmed by dollar appreciation while those with negative net export orientation potentially benefit thanks to cheaper inputs. Using Bureau of Economic Analysis input-output tables, trade data from the US International Trade Commission, and industry data from the Annual Survey of Manufactures, we apply Goldberg

Figure 6.7   Industrial exposure to a US oil and gas boom

net export orientation (percent)

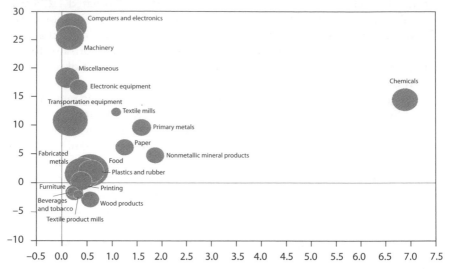

energy cost savings as a share of shipment value (percent)

Sources: Authors' calculations using the National Energy Modeling System; EIA (2013f); Census Bureau (2012); BEA (2013); Goldberg and Crockett (1998).

and Crockett's methodology to assess the net export orientation for the manufacturing industries included in the EIA's Manufacturing Energy Consumption Survey. Most energy-intensive industries have a relatively low or negative net export orientation. Exceptions include fertilizer, rubber, basic inorganic chemicals, and some food and nonferrous metal products (figure 6.7 and table 6.5). So as a group, energy-intensive manufacturing is unlikely to be significantly harmed, and could even be helped, by dollar appreciation resulting from an oil and gas production boom. But the net export exposure is higher in other manufacturing industries, such as electronics, aviation, and machinery—industries for which the potential reduction in production costs from cheaper energy is less than 1 percent. These industries could very well be harmed by an oil and gas renaissance, as studies on Dutch disease suggest.

Lower Energy Bills

While the effect of an oil and gas renaissance on US manufacturing will likely be mixed, the effects on household budgets is clearly positive. As discussed in chapter 4, increased consumption thanks to lower energy costs is the single largest economic benefit of increased oil and gas supply in our analysis. These gains, however, are not evenly spread.

Figure 6.8   US oil and gas expenditures as a share of personal income relative to urbanization, 2010

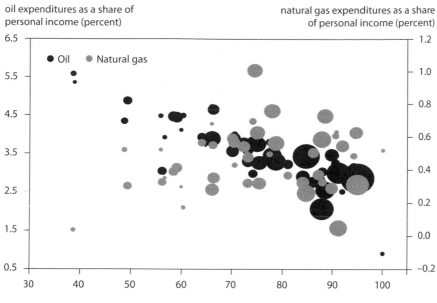

oil expenditures as a share of
personal income (percent)

natural gas expenditures as a share
of personal income (percent)

percent share of population in urban areas

Sources: EIA (2012e); BLS (2013d).

Regional differences in gasoline prices can arise from shifts in refinery economics and the distribution of domestic supply. Oil sands production in Canada and tight oil production in the Bakken have grown faster than the pipeline capacity needed to connect them to international markets. This led to a $40 difference in price in spring 2012 between Bakken and Canadian crude and similar-quality oil produced in the Gulf of Mexico.[9] The midcontinent refiners processing this oil passed relatively little of the cost savings onto consumers. And given oil's low cost of transportation relative to the value of the product, crude or refined product price dislocations are likely temporary in nature.

More persistent are regional differences in oil consumption. Households in rural states spend more of their income on oil than urban states because they drive farther and earn less money (figure 6.8). Rural states in New England—Maine, Vermont, and New Hampshire—use oil for home heating. Natural gas penetration, on the other hand, is higher in urban states, both on an absolute

---

9. Trevor Houser, "Gasoline Prices and Electoral Politics Part Two," Rhodium Group Note, March 20, 2012, http://rhgroup.net/notes/gasoline-prices-and-electoral-politics-part-two (accessed on September 8, 2013).

Figure 6.9 US potential household energy cost savings as a share of personal income

change in energy expenditures as a share of personal income (percent)

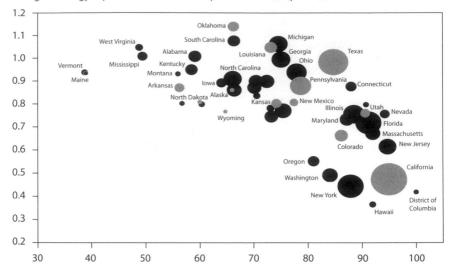

percent share of population in urban areas

Note: Bubble size denotes size of state's population.

Sources: EIA (2012e); BLS (2013d); authors' calculations using the Natural Energy Modeling System.

basis and as a share of personal income. Electricity is somewhere in between, because while urban residents use less and earn more than their rural counterparts, power prices in urban states are much higher. We applied the same approach for assessing the regional effect of continued growth in US oil and gas production as in the industrial analysis described above. The EIA breaks down energy consumption by state and fuel for 2010 (EIA 2012e). NEMS projects energy prices by fuel for the nine US census regions. We took the projected price difference between the pre-shale and optimistic scenarios for each census region and applied it to 2010 levels of energy consumption for the states within that region, shown on the y-axis of figure 6.9. The x-axis represents urbanization and bubble size represents population. Midwest and southern states see the largest declines in household energy expenditures as a share of income under our optimistic scenario, while the West Coast and East Coast, with the exception of rural New England, see the smallest gains. Rocky Mountain and Southwest states largely fall in the middle. States producing more than 250,000 boe/d of oil and gas during the first half of 2012 are marked in light grey.

Putting It Together

The net economic effects of the oil and gas boom on each state depend on the combination of factors described above. Exact estimates are extremely difficult, as we do not know for sure where future production will come from and the regional patterns of manufacturing and energy use change over time. But we can see where states sit on the spectrum today and identify those that likely have the most to gain. To do this, we assess each state's ranking on each of the three variables discussed above: direct oil and gas employment, exposure to manufacturing upside from higher demand and increased competitiveness, and decrease in household energy costs as a share of income. We then create normalized indexes, with 1 indicating the lowest benefit and 10 the highest.

For oil and gas employment, the index is an equal weighting of current oil and gas employment as a share of the state total and growth in that share between the first through third quarters of 2007 and the first through third quarters of 2012. For manufacturing, we looked at current employment in industries that would either see a greater than 5 percent increase in output thanks to oil and gas investment or a greater than 2 percent decrease in energy costs as a share of shipment value thanks to lower energy prices.[10] For household energy expenses, we use the reduction in household energy costs as a share of income metric described above.

Figure 6.10 displays the analysis results. The x-axis is the index of positively exposed state manufacturing employment as a share of the total. The y-axis is household energy savings as a share of income. The circle size indicates oil and gas employment and growth as a share of state totals. The circle shading indicates US census region. Oil and gas employment is most important to rural Western and Great Plains states, particularly Wyoming, New Mexico, Colorado, Alaska, and North Dakota. The Midwest is best positioned to benefit from any manufacturing benefits of the oil and gas boom, though some Midwestern states might see offsetting declines in more exchange rate–exposed manufacturing. The South sees the most significant household energy savings as a share of income. A handful of states, most located near the Gulf Coast, do well on all three variables. Oklahoma, Texas, and Louisiana stand out in particular, with a large oil and gas industry presence, significant household energy cost savings, and manufacturing sectors more positively exposed to lower energy costs or higher demand than negatively exposed to real effective exchange rate appreciation resulting from the oil and gas boom.

---

10. The level of manufacturing employment detail at the national level (see table 6.5) is not available for all states because of disclosure issues, so we aggregate from the 6-digit North American Industry Classification System (NAICS) level to the 4-digit NAICS level for some industries.

Figure 6.10 State-level oil and gas boom benefit indices

household expenditures as a share of income (percent)

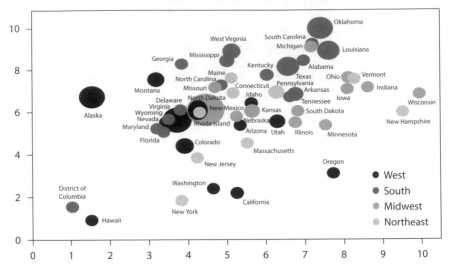

positively exposed manufacturing employment as a share of total (percent)

Note: Positively exposed manufacturing employment as a share of total (x axis), household energy savings as a share of income (y axis), and oil and gas employment and growth as a share of state totals (circle size). Bubble shading reflects US census region.

Sources: EIA (2012e, 2013f); Census Bureau (2012); BLS (2013b, 2013d); authors' calculations using the Natural Energy Modeling System.

7

Environmental Costs and Benefits

For all the recent excitement about the potential economic and national security benefits of the US oil and gas boom, there is equal, if not greater, concern
about its potential environmental consequences. The Deepwater Horizon oil
spill in the Gulf of Mexico in 2010 dominated national media for weeks on end,
the Keystone XL oil pipeline became a prominent issue in the 2012 presidential election, and protests against hydrofracking have become a regular part of
life in many energy-rich states. In the previous chapters we have attempted to
quantify the economic effects of the oil and gas boom. It is equally important
to quantify its environmental costs and benefits. A proper analysis is beyond
the scope of this book, but this chapter offers a brief discussion of the environmental implications of unconventional oil and gas development and how
policy can mitigate its negative effects.

Water, Air, and Earthquakes

Most of the environmental concern surrounding increased oil and gas development has focused on local effects in the communities where the development
is occurring, regarding water resources in particular. In addition to taking the
lives of eleven people, the Deepwater Horizon explosion significantly damaged
Gulf Coast ecosystems, including beaches, wetlands, and commercial fisheries.
And a couple of high-profile pipeline accidents in recent years have raised
concerns about onshore water contamination risks from oil and gas development.[1] But the potential effect of hydraulic fracturing, or fracking, on local
water supplies has received the most attention.

---

1. See, e.g., EPA, "EPA's Response to the Enbridge Oil Spill," www.epa.gov/enbridgespill (accessed
on September 8, 2013).

As discussed in chapter 2, fracking is performed by injecting pressurized water, sand, and additives into a wellbore to create fissures in semipermeable shale or tight gas reservoirs. This releases trapped natural gas, which, along with the fluid used to fracture the well, flows back up the wellbore. While shale and gas reservoirs are generally located between 3,000 and 12,000 feet below the surface, wells often pass through groundwater reservoirs before reaching shale (EIA 2011c). The wellbore is sealed in cement to protect groundwater supplies, but many environmental and community groups are concerned that the chemicals used in fracking could still find their way into local water supplies. Similar concerns surround wastewater disposal.

In 2008 the residents of Pavillion, Wyoming, began complaining about discolored and foul-smelling local water, prompting an Environmental Protection Agency (EPA) investigation. In 2011 the EPA issued a draft report concluding that contaminants found in the town's water likely came from nearby natural gas drilling (EPA 2011a).[2] Of the tens of thousands of gas wells that have been fracked in recent years, this was the first government finding of groundwater contamination, and it was from a tight gas rather than a shale gas well. Still, it has heightened public concern about the environmental costs of the oil and gas boom. Rather than fracking chemicals, methane—what natural gas is made of—has been found in the water supply in a number of areas where gas development is occurring (Osborn et al. 2011). This could be from the drilling process, or it could have naturally migrated into the water reservoir from the shale formation. Methane is not toxic, but it can be highly flammable—a characteristic most people generally do not look for in drinking water. The EPA is conducting a comprehensive study of the effects of fracking on drinking water and groundwater, to be completed in 2014. This assessment will likely serve as the scientific basis for any water-related federal regulation of fracking in the years ahead.

Water contamination is not the only concern surrounding the underground injection of fracking fluids or wastewater management. While the overwhelming majority of earthquakes have natural causes, some are attributable to human activity. These so-called induced seismic events have been documented since the 1920s and can be traced to activities ranging from coal mining to geothermal energy development. The vast majority of documented energy-related induced seismic events occurred due to geothermal development (NRC et al. 2012). But oil and gas extraction can induce seismic events as well if injection or withdrawal of fluids significantly alters subsurface pressure balances. Such occurrences are rare, and have been largely caused by enhanced oil recovery techniques, such as water flooding. Only one induced seismic event

---

2. The industry disputes many EPA draft report findings. See, e.g., Christopher Helman, "Questions Emerge on EPA's Wyoming Fracking Study," *Forbes*, December 9, 2011, www.forbes.com/sites/christopherhelman/2011/12/09/questions-emerge-on-epas-wyoming-fracking-study (accessed on September 8, 2013).

(2.8 magnitude) in the United States is suspected to have been caused by the injection of fracking fluids into a shale gas well, and one event in the United Kingdom has been conclusively linked to shale gas development. Of greater concern is the injection of wastewater, either from conventional or shale development, into disposal wells.

Finally, oil and gas development can create air quality problems in the communities where drilling is occurring. Diesel-powered trucks and drilling equipment emit particulate matter and sulfur dioxide, and oil and gas drilling—hydrofracking in particular—is a leading source of volatile organic compound emissions, which contribute to the formation of ground-level ozone.[3] Ozone exposure contributes to aggravated asthma and other respiratory illnesses. Oil and gas development also emits air toxics, such as benzene, ethylbenzene, and n-hexane, and studies have found high concentrations of airborne toxins near shale gas drilling sites (McKenzie et al. 2012). As unconventional gas development has accelerated, air quality complaints in communities in Wyoming, Texas, Pennsylvania, and other gas-rich states have become more prominent.[4]

Environmental Upside

The oil and gas boom is delivering environmental benefits as well as costs. While natural gas prices have plummeted in recent years, thanks to growth in shale and other unconventional supply, the price US power plants pay for coal has risen. Between 2000 and 2007, power plants paid $1.42 per million British thermal units (MMBtu), on average, for coal, compared with $5.81 for natural gas (EIA 2013d). During 2010 and 2011, delivered coal prices rose to an average of $2.30 per MMBtu while gas prices fell to $4.90, and in 2012, delivered coal and natural gas prices were $2.41 and $3.43 respectively, the smallest spread since the early 1970s (EIA 2013d).

As the gap between coal and natural gas prices narrowed, natural gas-fired power plants were able to outcompete coal-fired power plants in competitive wholesale markets in many parts of the country. A number of power companies started switching their generation portfolio away from coal to natural gas. As a result, coal's share of US power generation fell from 48 percent during 2008 to a record low of 32.6 percent in April 2012. Natural gas' share rose from 21 percent to 32.2 percent over the same period, coming close to overtaking coal as the leading source of power generation in the United States (EIA 2013d).

Burning natural gas emits fewer air pollutants, such as sulfur dioxide (SO_2), nitrogen oxide (NO_x), and mercury, than burning coal. Natural gas-fired power plants are also, on average, more efficient than their coal-fired peers, meaning

---

3. For more information, see EPA, "Oil and Natural Gas Air Pollution Standards," http://epa.gov/airquality/oilandgas/basic.html (accessed on September 8, 2013).

4. Kirk Johnson, "In Pinedale, Wyo., Residents Adjust to Air Pollution," *New York Times*, March 9, 2011.

that they need less fuel to generate the same amount of electricity. So with the power sector switching from coal to natural gas, US air pollution levels have fallen. The EPA estimates that between 2008 and 2012, US sulfur dioxide emissions fell by 15 percent per year, three times the average annual rate between 2000 and 2008 (EPA 2012c). The power sector accounted for 94 percent of this decline. It is difficult to assess exactly how much of this drop was due to coal-to-natural gas fuel switching, as power plants have other options for reducing SO_2 emissions, such as installing pollution control technology or switching to lower-sulfur coals. Slower power demand growth between 2008 and 2012 also played an important role. But the economic benefit of the overall reduction in power sector SO_2 emissions is significant. The National Research Council (NRC 2009) estimates that each ton of SO_2 emitted from a coal-fired power plant costs the United States \$5,800 in environmental and human health damages. At these numbers, the decline in power sector SO_2 emissions between 2008 and 2012 saves the country \$26 billion per year.

Switching from coal to natural gas in the power sector has had a smaller but also important effect on NO_x emissions (EPA 2012c). Between 2008 and 2012, NO_x emissions declined twice as fast as between 2000 and 2008, with the power sector accounting for 23 percent of the drop (the transportation sector is responsible for the rest). The NRC also estimates that each ton of NO_x emitted costs the country \$1,600. At that rate, the decline in power sector NO_x emissions between 2008 and 2012 saves the country an additional \$2 billion per year. Switching from coal to natural gas also lowers mercury and particulate matter pollution, but recent emissions data are not available.

Climate Breakthrough?

Beyond local air pollution reductions, the oil and gas boom has delivered some global environmental benefits as well. At the UN climate change summit in Copenhagen in 2009, the United States pledged to reduce greenhouse gas emissions 17 percent below 2005 levels by 2020 (Houser 2010). This pledge was conditioned on enactment of domestic cap-and-trade legislation that had passed the House of Representatives that spring (UNFCCC 2009). After the Copenhagen summit concluded, however, cap-and-trade legislation died in the Senate and never made it to President Obama's desk to sign. In the face of this legislative failure and the Republican takeover of the House of Representatives in 2010, environmental activists worried the United States would not be able to achieve its target and that other countries would moderate their emission reduction efforts in response.

Yet despite the absence of federal policy, US emissions have fallen sharply in recent years, raising hopes that the United States might still be able to reach its 2020 goal. In 2012, energy-related CO_2 emissions, which account for 79 percent of total US greenhouse gas (GHG) emissions, were 12 percent below 2005 levels (figure 7.1). That is a sharper decline than in the European Union, which has an economywide climate policy; there, CO_2 emissions in 2012 were

Figure 7.1   Energy-related CO_2 emissions, United States versus EU-27, 2000–12 (billions of tons)

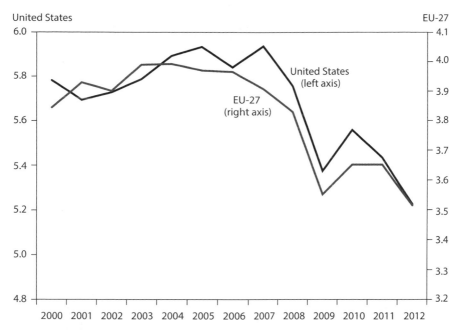

Note: 2012 figures are annualized estimates from first half data.

Sources: United Nations Framework Convention on Climate Change; EuroStat; Energy Information Administration.

down 10 percent from 2005 levels (figure 7.1).[5] It is also a dramatic departure from what most analysts, until recently, expected to occur. In 2006 the Energy Information Administration (EIA) forecast that energy-related CO_2 emissions in the United States would increase by 9 percent between 2005 and 2012 to 6,536 million tons (figure 7.2). Actual emissions in 2012 were 5,290 million tons, their lowest level since 1994.

What explains the unexpected drop? In the broadest terms, the amount of CO_2 a country emits is determined by the level of economic activity (measured in GDP), the amount of energy consumed per unit of GDP (energy intensity), and the amount of CO_2 emitted per unit of energy consumed (carbon intensity). A significant change in any one of these factors can alter a country's CO_2

---

5. The Europeans prefer to measure reductions against a 1990 baseline, the base year for Kyoto Protocol commitments. Against 1990 levels, US emissions were up by 7 percent in 2012, compared with a 13 percent decline for the European Union. Also, the EU Emissions Trading Scheme allows companies and countries to meet their compliance obligations by purchasing emissions reductions, called offsets, from other parts of the world instead of reducing emissions at home. Including offsets in the above calculation increases overall EU emissions reductions relative to the United States.

Figure 7.2   Actual energy-related US CO$_2$ emissions versus EIA 2006 projections, 1985–2012

millions of tons

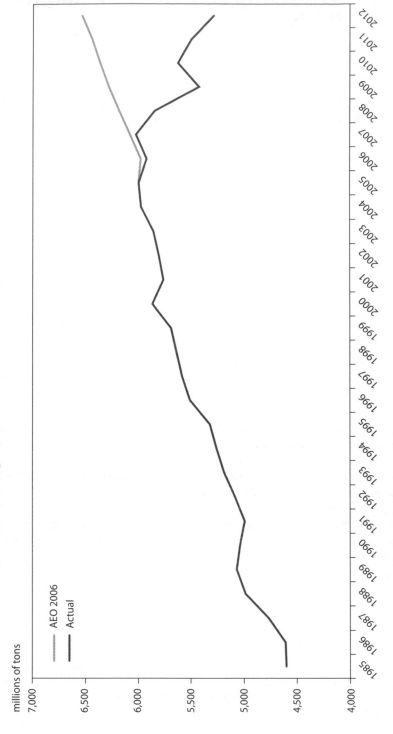

AEO 2006

Actual

EIA = Energy Information Administration; AEO = Annual Energy Outlook

Sources: EIA (2006, 2012b, 2013d).

Figure 7.3   Difference between actual CO$_2$ emissions in 2012 and EIA 2006 projections, by source of change

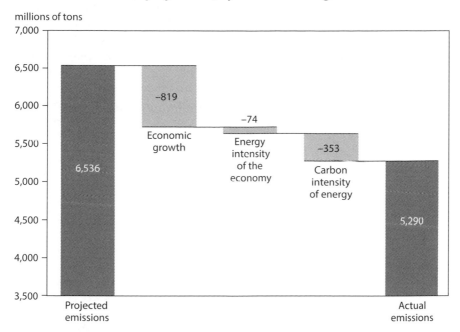

millions of tons

Sources: EIA (2006, 2013d).

emissions trajectory. The EIA projected in 2006 that the US economy would grow by 3.1 percent a year between 2005 and 2012, continuing its average rate of GDP growth between 1990 and 2005. The energy intensity of the economy was expected to decline by 1.65 percent a year, down a bit from the 1990–2005 annual average of 1.86 percent due primarily to a slowdown in the US economy's transition from manufacturing (more energy intensity) to service sector (less energy intensive) activity. The carbon intensity of energy supply was projected to remain the same, with the shares coming from coal, natural gas, oil, nuclear, and renewables holding relatively constant.

However, due to the financial crisis, the economy expanded much less than projected, with GDP growth averaging 1.1 percent between 2005 and 2012. That alone accounts for 66 percent of the difference between projected and actual emissions in 2012, or 819 million tons (figure 7.3).[6] Energy intensity

---

6. For this attribution, we adopt a similar methodology to the Council of Economic Advisers (CEA 2013) in their 2013 *Economic Report of the President*. CO$_2$ emissions are the product of (CO$_2$/BTU) × (BTU/GDP) × GDP, where CO$_2$ represents US CO$_2$ emissions in a given year, BTU represents energy consumption in that year, and GDP is that year's GDP. We take logarithms of this expression and subtract the baseline from the actual values to attribute reductions to slower economic growth, less energy-intensive economic activity, and lower carbon intensity of energy supply. The

declined faster than expected (1.80 percent per year instead of 1.65 percent) because of high energy prices and improved efficiency in vehicles, buildings, and industry. That accounts for 6 percent of the decline, or 74 million tons. The carbon intensity of energy supply fell to all-time lows, delivering the remaining 28 percent of the downside surprise in US emissions, or 353 million tons. Thus a number of developments between 2005 and 2012 contributed to the decline in the carbon intensity of US energy supply. As discussed in chapter 5, increased ethanol production allowed for fuel switching in the transportation sector. Ethanol and other biofuels emit CO_2 when they are produced and when they are combusted, but the plants used as feedstock also sequester CO_2 as they grow. Based on EIA data, fuel switching in the transportation sector accounted for nearly 15 percent of the reduction in the carbon intensity of overall US energy supply between 2005 and 2012.[7] Fuel switching in the industrial sector accounted for 7 percent of the economywide carbon intensity reductions, thanks primarily to biomass substituting for coal in industrial boilers.

The greatest shift, however, occurred in the electric power sector (figure 7.4), as the market share of coal—the most carbon-intensive fuel used in power generation—declined from 51 percent to 38.5 percent.[8] Oil, the power sector's second most carbon-intensive fuel source, saw its share of generation fall from 3 percent to 0.5 percent. Meanwhile, zero-carbon sources of power generation, such as nuclear and renewables, grew from 28.2 percent to 31.5 percent, thanks primarily to an increase in wind generation. Natural gas saw even bigger gains,

---

CEA findings are slightly different from ours for two reasons. First, the CEA uses projected 2012 emissions, as full-year data were not yet available at the time of publication. Second and more important, they use a lower GDP growth estimate in their business-as-usual projection than the 3.1 percent used in the EIA 2006 projections. This reflects recent academic and government estimates that potential GDP growth in the United States has slowed to 2.5 to 2.6 percent. This is the right approach for attributing how much of the decline in emissions was due to the recession, whereas our approach compares actual GDP growth with projected GDP growth, with the difference covering both the recession and slower potential GDP growth than forecast in 2006.

7. The EIA energy-related CO_2 emissions data on which figures 7.1 to 7.4 are based capture the emissions released in the conversion of corn, sugar, oil, or other feedstock to biofuels, provided it occurs domestically, but in the industrial, not transportation, sector data. This is similar to petroleum products, where the emissions from gasoline combustion are included in the transportation sector data but emissions from crude oil refining are included in the industrial sector. A proper accounting of the net emissions effect of switching from petroleum to biofuels should include the emissions involved in producing both fuels, as well as combusting them, and would likely change the sectoral distribution of carbon-intensity reductions shown in figure 7.4. More important, EIA energy-related CO_2 data exclude emissions from biofuels combustion, assuming that the production of biofuel feedstocks sequesters an equal quantity of CO_2. While narrowly correct, increased biofuel production can lead to broader land-use change that could lead to a net decline in forest sequestration, offsetting some of the emissions benefit of switching from petroleum to ethanol or biodiesel. The EIA does not include land-use change estimates in either the overall or transport sector CO_2 data.

8. Generation in the electric power sector only. Data taken from EIA (2013d, table 7.2b).

Figure 7.4   Reduction in the carbon intensity of primary energy consumption, by sector, 2012 versus 2005

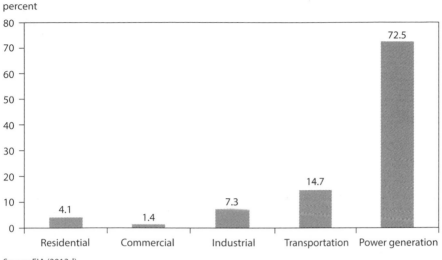

percent

Source: EIA (2013d).

growing from 17.5 percent of generation in 2005 to 29.2 percent in 2012 (EIA 2012d).

Switching from coal to natural gas for power generation has less of an effect on CO_2 emissions than on SO_2, NO_x and mercury pollution. While less carbon intensive than coal or oil, natural gas combustion still emits meaningful quantities of CO_2 while emitting very little NO_x and almost no SO_2 or mercury. On average, coal-fired power generation in the United States emits 2,249 pounds per megawatt hours (lbs/MWh) of carbon dioxide, 13 lbs/MWh of sulfur dioxide, and 6 lbs/MWh of nitrogen oxides. Natural gas-fired power generation emits 1,135 lbs/MWh of CO_2, 0.1 lbs/MWh of SO_2, and 1.7 lbs/MWh of NO_x.[9]

Determining exactly how much of the decline in the carbon intensity of US power generation is attributable to natural gas is challenging. For a rough estimate, we proportionally allocated the decline in coal's and oil's market shares in the electric power sector, and associated CO_2 emissions, between 2005 and 2012 to natural gas, nuclear, and renewables, based on the growth in each fuel's market share over the same period, factoring in CO_2 emissions from natural gas generation. Based on this approach, expanded use of natural gas accounted for 65 percent of the decarbonization of the power sector between 2005 and 2012, followed by wind at 30 percent, with nonwind renewables accounting for the rest. This approach, however, assumes that a kilowatt hour (kWh) displaced

9. EPA, "Air Emissions," www.epa.gov/cleanenergy/energy-and-you/affect/air-emissions.html (accessed on September 8, 2013).

by additional natural gas generation has the same carbon intensity as a kWh displaced by renewable generation. In reality, there are important regional differences in the competition between and dispatch profiles of different fuels, which a more robust attribution analysis would account for.[10] But it is safe to say that while the recession accounted for most of the decline in US emissions between 2005 and 2012, decarbonization of the power sector played an important role, and that was primarily due to low-cost natural gas.

Limits of Cheap Natural Gas

Emission reductions driven by cheap gas alone, however, appear to have run their course. While coal-fired power hit a record low of 33 percent of total US generation in April 2012 thanks to a shale-driven decline in natural gas costs, prices recovered during the second half of the year. By the end of 2012, the price of natural gas delivered to US power plants was up 57 percent and coal's market share had climbed back to 40 percent (EIA 2013d). A relatively cold winter continued to put upward pressure on natural gas prices into 2013, keeping coal competitive in the power sector. And overall electricity demand is growing slightly due to continued, though painfully slow, economic recovery. In its most recent short-term energy outlook as of the time of writing, the EIA predicted that US CO_2 emissions will rise by 3 percent in 2013.

Over the longer term, our modeling suggests that should more optimistic production forecasts pan out, the oil and gas boom will help keep power sector emissions growth in check but have only a modest net effect on US emissions overall. In our pre-shale scenario, coal maintains a 42 to 43 percent share of US power generation throughout the projection period (table 7.1 and figure 7.5). Overall power demand grows by just under 20 percent between 2013 and 2035, and coal-fired power generation moves with it. In our conservative scenario, coal's market share declines to 38 percent by 2016 and holds steady in percentage terms through 2035, resulting in modest absolute growth. In our optimistic case, however, coal-fired power generation falls from 1,734 billion kWh in 2011 to 1,285 billion kWh in 2016, then grows at half the rate of power generation overall. As a result, coal's share falls to 30 percent by 2020 and 28 percent by 2035.

Natural gas picks up the slack, with generation doubling between 2011 and 2035. By 2035 natural gas accounts for 40 percent of all power generation in our optimistic scenario, compared with 17 percent in the pre-shale case. Some of this growth comes at the expense of nuclear and renewables as well as coal. Nuclear generation grows by 7 percent between 2011 and 2035 in our

---

10. For a discussion of this point, see Trevor Houser, "More on the Recent US Emissions Decline," Rhodium Group, March 4, 2013, http://rhg.com/notes/more-on-the-recent-us-emissions-decline (accessed on September 8, 2013) and Michael Shellenberger, Ted Nordhaus, Alex Trembath, and Max Luke, "Debunking Rhodium," Breakthrough Institute, http://thebreakthrough.org/index.php/debunking-rhodium/ (accessed on September 8, 2013).

Table 7.1 Energy-sector implications of the oil and gas boom

| | Pre-shale | | | | | | Conservative | | | | Optimistic | | | |
| | 2011 | | 2020 | | 2035 | | 2020 | | 2035 | | 2020 | | 2035 | |
Source	Quantity	Percent	Quantity	Percent	Quantity	Percent	Quantity	Percent	Quantity	Percent	Quantity	Percent	Quantity	Percent
Energy consumption (quadrillion British thermal units)	97.3	100.0	98.5	100.0	106.0	100.0	99.4	100.0	106.8	100.0	100.2	100.0	108.4	100.0
Coal	19.6	20.2	20.8	21.1	23.1	21.8	18.8	18.9	21.1	19.8	14.8	14.7	16.2	15.0
Oil	35.3	36.3	34.4	34.9	33.6	31.7	34.7	34.9	34.0	31.9	35.3	35.2	34.9	32.2
Natural gas	24.8	25.5	23.4	23.8	22.2	20.9	26.1	26.2	27.3	25.6	30.5	30.5	33.7	31.1
Nuclear	8.3	8.5	9.3	9.4	11.1	10.5	9.3	9.3	9.3	8.7	9.0	9.0	8.9	8.2
Renewables	9.1	9.4	10.4	10.5	15.7	14.8	10.3	10.3	14.9	13.9	10.3	10.3	14.5	13.4
Power generation (billion kilowatt hours)	4,106	100.0	4,280	100.0	4,844	100.0	4,333	100.0	4,979	100.0	4,403	100.0	5,118	100.0
Coal	1,734	42.2	1,867	43.6	2,086	43.1	1,674	38.6	1,392	38.0	1,301	29.5	1,436	28.1
Oil	28	0.7	29	0.7	30	0.6	29	0.7	30	0.6	29	0.7	30	0.6
Natural gas	1,017	24.8	851	19.9	804	16.6	1,111	25.6	1,396	28.0	1,570	35.7	2,053	40.1
Nuclear	790	19.2	887	20.7	1,062	21.9	887	20.5	885	17.8	862	19.6	849	16.6
Renewables	520	12.7	626	14.6	842	17.4	612	14.1	755	15.2	620	14.1	729	14.2

Source: EIA (2013d); authors' calculations using the National Energy Modeling System.

Figure 7.5   Power generation by source under current policy, 2011–35

a. Pre-shale

billion kilowatt hours (percent share in shaded areas)

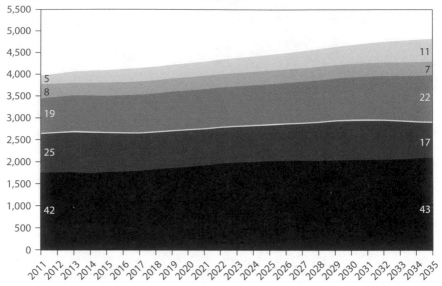

b. Optimistic

billion kilowatt hours (percent share in shaded areas)

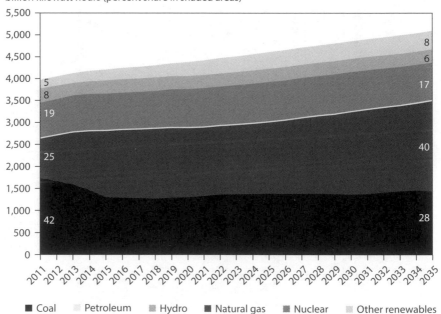

■ Coal   ▨ Petroleum   ■ Hydro   ■ Natural gas   ■ Nuclear   ▨ Other renewables

Source: Authors' calculations using the National Energy Modeling System.

Figure 7.6   Reduction in average annual emissions from power generation relative to pre-shale scenario, 2013–35

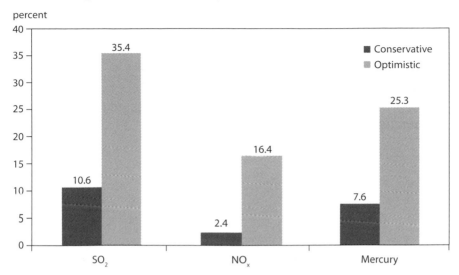

percent

Source: Authors' calculation using the National Energy Modeling System.

optimistic scenario, compared with 34 percent in the pre-shale case. Renewable generation still experiences a healthy 40 percent expansion between 2011 and 2035, but that is down from 62 percent in the pre-shale scenario (table 7.1). That means that by 2035 renewables account for 9 percent of total power generation instead of 11 percent.

That natural gas displaces some nuclear and renewables is not so bad from a local air pollution standpoint, as long as it is also displacing coal. Between 2013 and 2035 annual SO_2 emissions from the electric power sector are 10.6 percent and 35.4 percent lower on average in our conservative and optimistic scenarios compared with the pre-shale case (figure 7.6). NO_x emissions are 2.4 percent and 16.4 percent lower, while mercury emissions are 7.6 and 25.3 percent lower. In the pre-shale scenario SO_2, NO_x, and mercury emissions are already projected to decline, thanks to already adopted EPA regulations. Still, the difference in power sector SO_2 and NO_x emissions between the optimistic and pre-shale scenarios would deliver nearly $6 billion a year in additional economic savings using the NRC's damage estimates, and likely several billion more in annual savings from lower mercury emissions.

For CO_2, however, the long-term effect of the oil and gas boom is more modest. In our projections, there is little difference in US CO_2 emissions between the pre-shale and conservative scenarios, and in the optimistic scenario CO_2 emissions are only 109 million tons lower on average between 2013 and 2035 than in the pre-shale case (figure 7.7). Natural gas generation displaces some nuclear and renewables, as well as coal, which blunts its climate benefit

Figure 7.7   Energy-related CO$_2$ emissions, 1970–2035

billions of tons

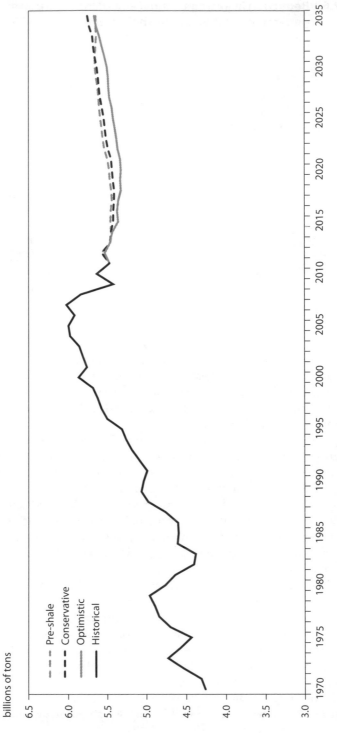

Sources: EIA (2012b); authors' calculations using the National Energy Modeling System.

Figure 7.8   Change in energy-related CO$_2$ emissions from the US oil and gas boom, 2013–35

millions of tons (annual average)

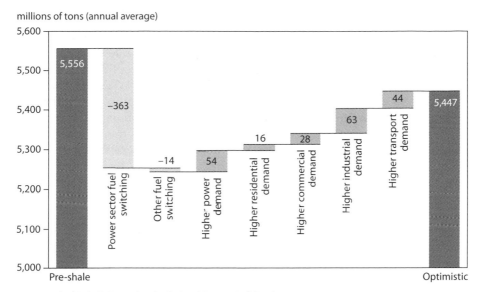

Source: Authors' calculations using the National Energy Modeling System.

(natural gas is a larger source of CO$_2$ emissions than SO$_2$, NO$_x$, or mercury emissions). But fuel switching in the power sector still delivers 363 million tons in average annual emission reductions in the optimistic scenario (figure 7.8). Fuel switching in other sectors adds an additional 14 million tons for a combined 377 million tons of abatement.

Energy analysts in recent years have actively debated the extent to which the environmental benefits of energy efficiency improvements are offset by increased energy demand (Jenkins, Nordhaus, and Shellenberger 2011; Gillingham et al. 2013). The rebound effect, as the phenomenon is known, occurs when, say, technical or design advances that improve the efficiency of cars, factories, and buildings lower the cost of energy services for consumers and thus lead to greater consumption of those services. If a rebound effect occurs when energy services are made cheaper through efficiency, it should also occur if energy services are made cheaper through lower-cost fossil fuels. Indeed, we see this in our modeling (figure 7.8). Lower natural gas prices mean lower electricity prices and thus power demand rises. Lower natural gas prices and increased competitiveness of energy-intensive manufacturing raise industrial energy demand as well. And as discussed in chapter 3, the shale boom is not confined to natural gas; it has spread to oil as well, resulting in modestly cheaper crude oil and refined petroleum products. That leads to higher oil demand and higher emissions in the transport sector. Finally, the increase in GDP discussed in chapter 4 raises energy demand across the economy. All told, lower energy prices and faster economic growth offset 71 percent of the CO_2 emission reductions achieved from natural gas-led fuel switching in the optimistic vs. pre-shale scenarios.

Other Considerations

Further complicating the picture, CO_2 is only one of the greenhouse gases that contribute to global climate change. CO_2 is the largest source of US GHG emissions, accounting for 84 percent of the total, with energy-related CO_2 emissions accounting for 79 percent (EPA 2013). Methane accounts for another 9 percent of total US GHG emissions, and according to EPA estimates, 25 percent of that comes from the production, transformation, and transportation of natural gas. Methane is what natural gas is made of, but when combusted it turns into CO_2. However, uncombusted methane that is released from natural gas systems, known as fugitive emissions, is 25 times as potent from a global warming standpoint as CO_2.[11]

In 2011 researchers at Cornell University estimated that fugitive emissions from shale gas production were much higher than those from conventional gas production—between 3.6 and 7.9 percent of total natural gas output—and that, as a result, the life cycle emissions associated with natural gas–fired power generation were comparable to electricity produced from coal over the long term and more harmful for the climate over the short term (Howarth, Santoro, and Ingraffea 2011).[12] In 2012, using field data from Colorado shale plays, researchers from the University of Colorado and the National Oceanic and Atmospheric Administration (NOAA) estimated leakage rates of 2.3 to 7.7 percent with a best guess of 4 percent (Pétron et al. 2012). This also suggested that from a climate standpoint, natural gas might not be better than coal.

Both studies have attracted considerable criticism, however. A number of scholars have taken issue with the leakage assumptions used in the Cornell study (Bradbury et al. 2013) and Michael Levi of the Council on Foreign Relations has highlighted significant methodological problems in the University of Colorado/NOAA estimates (Levi 2012c). Recent work from researchers at Carnegie Mellon University, the National Energy Technology Laboratory, Argonne National Laboratory, and the University of Texas estimates that shale gas leakage rates are comparable with conventional natural gas and that life cycle emissions from natural gas–fired power generation are 20 to 50 percent lower than coal-fired power generation depending on thermal efficiency levels (Bradbury et al. 2013). In its 2013 GHG emissions inventory, the EPA esti-

---

11. Measured using the 100-year global warming potential (GWP) of methane versus CO_2. The GWP is a measure of the climate effect of a greenhouse gas over a specific period of time compared with CO_2.

12. Long-term estimates are based on a 100-year GWP. Because methane is short-lived, its effect is front-loaded. Using a 20-year GWP, methane is 72 times more potent then CO_2. This is important if policymakers are concerned about exceeding climate tipping points or about the pace of warming in the short term.

mated an economywide methane leakage rate from natural gas systems of less than 1.5 percent,[13] similar to what Levi finds using the University of Colorado/NOAA data but correcting for their most prominent methodological error. At this level, natural gas is considerably more climate friendly than coal for power generation in both the short and long term.

While the high-end estimates from the Cornell and University of Colorado/NOAA studies appear to be outliers, there has still been relatively little direct measurement of fugitive emissions from shale or conventional oil and gas production. Existing studies have relied on data from a specific region or the EPA inventory, which has limited access to directly measured air emissions data and relies on indirect calculations informed by voluntarily supplied industry data (Bradbury et al. 2013). The EPA now requires methane emission reporting under the Greenhouse Gas Reporting Program for facilities that emit more than 25,000 metric tons of CO_2 or other GHGs per year, but does not yet require direct measurement. The Environmental Defense Fund and researchers from the University of Texas have launched a large-scale field study of fugitive emissions, which should provide better empirical data over the next couple of years.[14] Initial findings from this study were published in the *Proceedings of the National Academy of Sciences* in September 2013 and found leakage rates in line with the EPA inventory estimates (Allen et al. 2013).

Finally, oil and gas production changes in the US will affect GHG emissions in other countries as well. To the extent that higher US oil output lowers oil prices, it does so for everyone, which results in increased oil demand globally, not only in the United States. At the same time, lower US natural gas imports and the prospect of meaningful natural gas exports reduce the cost of gas in the rest of the world, making it more competitive with coal in China, India, and elsewhere. All else equal, this should reduce CO_2 emissions outside the United States. And as US coal producers see their domestic market erode thanks to low-cost natural gas, they are increasingly looking to export to consumers overseas. Environmental groups worry this could offset the climate benefit of a coal-to-gas switch at home and greater supply of US liquefied natural gas (LNG) abroad. We discuss these trade-related environmental considerations in depth in chapter 8.

Why Policy Matters

On balance, the oil and gas boom is neither the environmental savior that industry proponents claim nor the existential threat that many in the environmental community see. Good policy can successfully mitigate the environmental risks discussed above. The water, air, and seismic consequences of unconventional oil and gas development are not intrinsic to the process.

---

13. Calculated using methodology laid out in Bradbury et al. (2013).

14. Environmental Defense Fund, "What Will It Take to Get Sustained Benefits from Natural Gas?" www.edf.org/methaneleakage (accessed on September 8, 2013).

They can be controlled by industry best practices and smart regulation. The United States captured the benefits of steel production and electricity generation during the last century while reducing their environmental consequences, and at much lower cost than originally believed possible. Likewise, the IEA estimates that the implementation of golden rules addressing the local environmental consequences of unconventional gas development—whether voluntarily adopted by industry or imposed by government—would raise costs by only 7 percent (IEA 2012c). Given that natural gas prices fall by between 25 and 60 percent in our analysis as a result of the shale boom, a 7 percent rebound is pretty modest.

Industry and government are already working to put such golden rules in place. A number of natural gas producers have begun voluntarily disclosing the chemicals used in their fracking operations, and a number of states have made such disclosures mandatory (McKenzie et al. 2012). The federal government has issued rules to address the emission of volatile organic compounds, air toxins, and methane from oil and gas production (EPA 2012c). The World Resources Institute estimates that these rules will reduce GHG emissions from upstream shale gas production by 40 to 46 percent and that the widespread application of three currently available cost-effective technologies could reduce fugitive emissions by another 30 percent (Bradbury et al. 2013). As mentioned above, the EPA is in the final stages of a multiyear review of the environmental effect of unconventional oil and gas development that will guide additional rulemaking.

At the same time, the potential environmental benefits of the oil and gas boom cannot be realized without policy help. Future reductions in SO_2, NO_x, and mercury emissions discussed above are meaningful but fairly small compared with the effect of recently enacted pollution control regulations. For CO_2 emissions, most of the low-hanging fruit has already been picked. By itself, the oil and gas boom does little to reduce emissions down the road. It does, however, make emission reduction policy cheaper and potentially more politically attractive.

We analyzed the effect of a modest carbon price on US energy costs, expenditures, and emissions under our pre-shale, conservative, and optimistic scenarios. Such a carbon price could be imposed through a tax, which has gotten some attention recently as part of the broader tax reform debate; a clean energy standard proposed in the president's 2011 State of the Union address; cap-and-trade legislation like that passed by the House of Representatives in 2009; or EPA regulations on new and existing power plants. Each of these policy instruments has unique design elements that shape the way it affects the energy sector. A clean energy standard covers the electric power sector only, as do the EPA regulations mentioned above. The cap-and-trade bill passed by the House in 2009 gave companies the ability to reduce emissions abroad as well as at home. The way we applied a carbon price is most similar to a potential carbon tax that rises gradually over time and covers all sectors of the economy.[15] But the ways in which the oil and gas boom have changed the cost and politics of pricing carbon apply to all four mechanisms described above.

In our pre-shale scenario, a $15 per ton carbon price rising at an inflation-adjusted rate of 5 percent per year reduces annual CO_2 emissions by 488 million tons per year in 2020 and 1,082 million tons per year in 2035 (figures 7.9 and 7.10 and table 7.2). That happens primarily through a shift from coal to nuclear and renewables in the power sector. In our optimistic scenario, low-cost natural gas provides a cheaper abatement opportunity and a carbon price extends and accelerates the recent coal-to-gas switch. CO_2 emissions in 2020 are 225 million tons below where they would have been in a pre-shale world with the same carbon price, or 20.6 percent below 2005 levels as opposed to 16.8 percent. This is despite faster economic growth and energy demand in the optimistic scenario.

In the pre-shale scenario, a $15 per ton carbon price raises residential electricity prices by 1.9 cents per kWh on average between 2013 and 2035 relative to where they would have been without a carbon price in place (table 7.3). Because of low-cost natural gas, the increase in the optimistic scenario is only 1.6 cents per kWh. More importantly, US GDP is higher and household energy expenditures are lower in the optimistic scenario with a carbon price than in a pre-shale world without a carbon price. The US economy is $252 billion larger, on average, between 2013 and 2035 thanks to the increase in oil and gas production in the optimistic case. A $15 per ton carbon price would only offset a third of these gains and deliver important environmental cost savings as a result. Oil and natural gas prices would still be considerably lower with a carbon price than in a pre-shale world and residential electricity prices would be roughly the same.

On the producer side, the oil and gas boom makes a carbon price more attractive as well. In a pre-shale world, the most cost-effective pathway to reduce CO_2 emissions was to switch from coal-fired power generation to renewables and nuclear (table 7.2 and figure 7.10). The political challenge of this solution was that, while the losers of such a policy were well known (e.g., coal producers and coal consumers), the winners had yet to be born (e.g., nuclear and renewable equipment manufacturers and installers). Take Texas as an example, which relies on coal shipped in from the Powder River Basin in Wyoming to generate a large share of its electricity. In a pre-shale world, pricing carbon would have raised the cost of electricity to the state's residents with no assurance that the renewable or nuclear technology used to replace coal would be made by in-state companies. Given the number of states that rely on coal for power generation and their combined power in the US Senate, this kind of local economic math made passing climate legislation extremely difficult.

---

15. Our carbon price begins at $15 per ton in 2013 and rises at an inflation-adjusted rate of 5 percent per year through 2035.

Figure 7.9 Energy-related CO_2 emissions under a \$15 per ton carbon price, 1970–2035

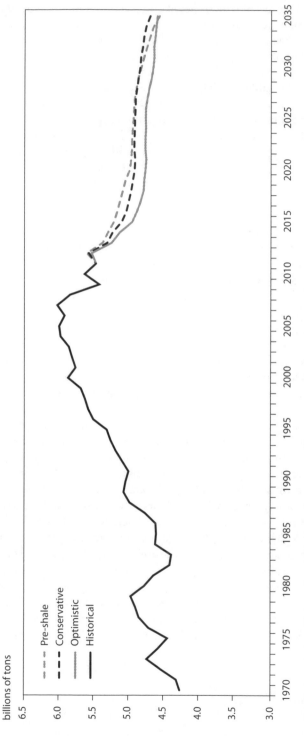

billions of tons

Pre-shale
Conservative
Optimistic
Historical

Note: Carbon price is applied economywide in 2013 at \$15 per ton and increases at an inflation-adjusted rate of 5 percent per year.

Sources: EIA (2012b); authors' calculations using the National Energy Modeling System.

Figure 7.10   Power generation by source with a carbon price, 2011–35

a. Pre-shale with carbon price

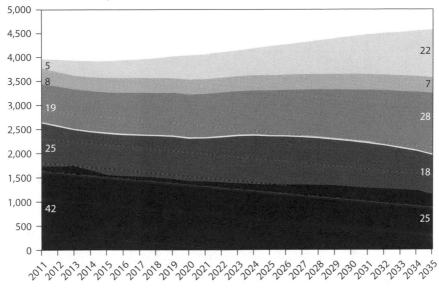

b. Optimistic with carbon price

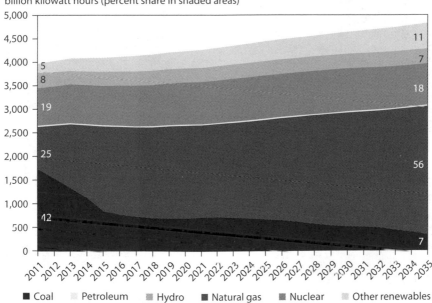

Note: Carbon price is applied economywide in 2013 at $15 per ton and increases at an inflation-adjusted rate of 5 percent per year.

Source: Authors' calculations using the National Energy Modeling System.

Table 7.2 Combining a carbon price with the oil and gas boom

Source	Pre-shale 2020 Without CO$_2$ price	Pre-shale 2020 With CO$_2$ price	Pre-shale 2035 Without CO$_2$ price	Pre-shale 2035 With CO$_2$ price	Optimistic 2020 Without CO$_2$ price	Optimistic 2020 With CO$_2$ price	Optimistic 2035 Without CO$_2$ price	Optimistic 2035 With CO$_2$ price
Energy consumption								
Coal (million short tons)	1,085.0	828.7	1,237.0	687.6	763.5	434.6	865.0	274.8
Oil (million barrels per day)	17.3	17.3	16.6	16.0	17.9	17.7	17.5	16.9
Natural gas (trillion cubic feet)	22.9	22.8	21.6	21.6	29.8	31.5	32.9	35.9
Nuclear (quadrillion British thermal units)	9.3	9.3	11.1	13.2	9.0	9.3	8.9	9.2
Renewables (quadrillion British thermal units)	10.4	12.3	15.7	21.9	10.3	10.8	14.5	16.4
Power generation (percent of total)								
Coal	43.6	34.5	43.1	24.9	29.5	16.2	28.1	7.0
Oil	0.7	0.7	0.6	0.6	0.7	0.6	0.6	0.5
Natural gas	19.9	22.9	16.6	17.6	35.7	46.1	40.1	56.1
Nuclear	20.7	21.5	21.9	27.6	19.6	20.8	16.6	18.1
Renewables	14.6	19.9	17.4	29.3	14.1	15.7	14.2	17.9
Environment								
CO$_2$ emissions (energy-related, billions of tons)	5,475	4,987	5,646	4,564	5,326	4,762	5,668	4,594
SO$_2$ emissions (power sector, millions of tons)	1.6	1.2	1.8	0.9	0.9	0.6	1.0	0.3
NO$_x$ emissions (power sector, millions of tons)	1.9	1.5	2.0	1.2	1.5	0.9	1.7	0.6
Mercury emissions (power sector, tons)	7.5	5.8	8.5	4.9	5.1	2.9	5.8	1.5

Note: Carbon price is applied economywide in 2013 at $15 per ton and increases at an inflation-adjusted rate of 5 percent per year.

Source: Authors' calculations using the National Energy Modeling System.

Table 7.3 Annual average producer revenue and consumer expenditures, 2013–35

	Pre-shale		Conservative		Optimistic	
	Without CO$_2$ price	With CO$_2$ price	Without CO$_2$ price	With CO$_2$ price	Without CO$_2$ price	With CO$_2$ price
Fossil fuel production						
Coal (million short tons)	1,186.10	882.20	1,096.70	770.00	895.00	523.50
Oil (million barrels per day)	7.80	8.00	9.20	9.40	13.00	13.20
Natural gas (trillion cubic feet)	21.60	21.10	25.70	26.50	31.30	32.90
Annual producer revenues (billions of 2010 US dollars)						
Coal	53.20	43.40	48.50	38.30	39.50	28.20
Oil	376.20	381.80	429.30	425.00	529.20	526.70
Natural gas	144.50	161.40	127.20	145.60	90.50	114.40
Energy prices and expenditures (2010 US dollars)						
Residential electricity prices (cents per kilowatt hour)	12.20	14.10	11.70	13.30	10.80	12.40
Gasoline prices (US dollars per gallon)	3.90	4.10	3.80	4.00	3.50	3.70
Natural gas prices (Henry Hub, US dollars per million British thermal units)	7.40	8.50	5.40	6.10	3.10	3.80
Average industrial energy price (US dollars per million British thermal units)	16.10	18.60	14.90	17.00	12.80	14.90
Household energy expenditures (2010 US dollars per household)	5,342.10	5,712.30	5,160.20	5,477.10	4,800.30	5,133.50
Macroeconomic						
GDP (trillions of 2005 chained US dollars)	18.79	18.73	18.87	18.79	19.04	18.96
Employment (nonfarm, million people)	152.10	152.00	152.60	152.40	153.60	153.40

Note: Carbon price is applied economywide in 2013 at $15 per ton and increases at an inflation-adjusted rate of 5 percent per year.

Source: Authors' calculations using the National Energy Modeling System.

Coal consumption declines faster in the presence of a carbon price under either the conservative or optimistic scenario than in the pre-shale case, but natural gas makes up the difference instead of nuclear and renewables (table 7.2 and figure 7.10). This increase in natural gas demand raises prices. The combined effect is a 14 to 26 percent increase in natural gas production revenue on average between 2013 and 2035 (table 7.3). Domestic oil production actually increases with a carbon price—between 148,000 and 175,000 barrels per day (bbl/d)—as more CO_2 is available for enhanced oil recovery. On the whole, oil and gas producer revenue increases by $14.2 billion to $21.4 billion per year between 2013 and 2035. Coal producer revenue declines by between $10.2 billion and $11.3 billion per year—leaving fossil fuel producers as a group better off with a carbon price than without. This potentially changes the political math of climate change policy. In a post-shale world, a carbon price moves Texas and a number of other states away from coal mined elsewhere in the country to natural gas produced in their own backyard. This, along with a smaller electricity price increase thanks to low-cost natural gas, could potentially make pricing carbon (either through legislation or regulation) more politically attractive in gas-rich parts of the country. And as the shale boom has spread, gas-producing states are increasingly outnumbering coal-producing states. Even in Pennsylvania, a long-time coal powerhouse, more people are employed in the oil and gas industry.

While low-cost natural gas makes reducing CO_2 emissions cheaper and more politically attractive in the short and medium term, achieving the long-term emission reductions required to address climate change will require moving from natural gas to nuclear and renewables, or equipping natural gas-fired power plants with carbon capture and sequestration.[16] The problem is that on a cost basis alone, nuclear and renewables will have a difficult time competing with natural gas over the next decade. Lower renewable and nuclear deployment in the short and medium term means higher costs in the long term, making future mitigation more difficult. Policymakers can address this by using some of the tax revenue generated through higher oil and gas royalty and lease revenue, or hypothetically carbon tax revenue were such legislation to pass, to fund nuclear and renewable research, development, and deployment and help foster further progress in these technologies.

---

16. See, for example, Michael A. Levi, 2012, "The Climate Change Limits of U.S. Natural Gas," Council on Foreign Relations, August 20, 2012, http://blogs.cfr.org/levi/2012/08/20/the-climate-change-limits-of-u-s-natural-gas.

8

Trade Policy Considerations

The rapidly changing energy landscape in the United States is forcing policymakers to reevaluate some long-held ideas about international trade. Since the founding of the postwar global trading system, the United States has been a leading proponent of open trade. For most of that time the country was a net energy importer, so access to international energy and natural resource supplies was an important trade policy priority. With the ever-elusive policy goal of energy independence now potentially within reach, at least from an accounting standpoint, some in Washington are questioning the benefits of open international energy trade. Will selling US natural gas abroad raise prices at home and undermine the country's newfound energy cost advantage? Will exporting US oil make the United States less energy secure? Will exporting domestic coal supply, freed up thanks to greater use of natural gas in power generation, undermine recent declines in US CO_2 emissions?

Natural Gas

As discussed in previous chapters, natural gas is leading the current US fossil fuel boom. It is also at the forefront of the emerging energy trade policy debate. Not long ago, the United States was the world's largest natural gas importer. At just over 10 billion cubic feet per day (Bcfd) in 2007, net imports accounted for 16 percent of US natural gas consumption (figure 8.1). That year, the United States imported 1 Bcfd more than Japan and 3 Bcfd more than Germany, the second and third largest gas importers (BP 2013). Most US gas imports were supplied through a pipeline from Canada, but the United States was also projected to become one of the largest importers of liquefied natural gas (LNG). In 2007 the Energy Information Administration (EIA) projected net US natural

Figure 8.1 Natural gas net imports as a share of demand, 1985–2012

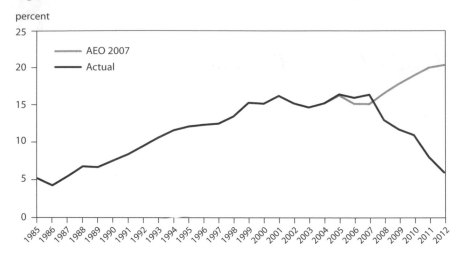

percent

AEO = Annual Energy Outlook

Sources: EIA (2007, 2012b, 2013d).

gas imports increasing to 14 Bcfd by 2012, with LNG accounting for roughly half (EIA 2007). It also forecast that, by 2020, US LNG imports alone would grow to 10 Bcfd, more than 25 percent of the current global LNG market and more than Japan, the world's largest LNG customer, purchased in 2007. New or expanded LNG import terminals were planned along the East Coast and Gulf of Mexico, supported by the federal government (Ebinger, Massy, and Avasarala 2012).

By 2012, however, net US natural gas imports had fallen to 4.1 Bcfd, half Japanese levels and less than Germany or Italy. Net imports accounted for only 6 percent of total consumption, compared with the 20 percent forecast by the EIA in 2007 (figure 8.1). The industry is now looking at exporting domestic natural gas in the form of LNG, in many cases using the same terminals that were built for imports, and global gas consumers are salivating at the prospect that US supply might reduce Qatar's and Australia's dominance of the global LNG market.

In 2007, US natural gas prices at Henry Hub were on par with European or Japanese import prices. Five years later, Henry Hub prices were less than one-third of European levels and less than one-fifth of Japanese levels (BP 2013). The average spread between US Henry Hub and Japanese LNG import prices in 2012 was more than $13 per million British thermal units (MMBtu). The IEA estimates that liquefaction and transport of LNG from the US Gulf Coast to Japan cost $8 to $9 per MMBtu at current LNG shipping rates, which leaves a healthy $4 to $6 per MMBtu arbitrage opportunity—hence the interest in US exports by both US industry and foreign LNG buyers (IEA 2012b). In addition, for its Sabine Pass terminal—the most advanced LNG export project in the United States—Cheniere, a US energy company, has signed supply agreements with customers linked to Henry Hub prices, as opposed to nearly all current LNG trade, which is linked to the price of crude oil. For buyers, this can provide welcome portfolio diversification and holds the promise of eroding an oil-linked pricing system that Japan and other large LNG importers see as excessively expensive given the currently high oil price.

While the current economics of LNG exports are compelling, there are potential policy barriers to shipping US natural gas abroad. Under the Natural Gas Act of 1938, anyone wishing to import natural gas into the United States or export it from the United States must receive approval from the Department of Energy (DOE).[1] The DOE must find that such importation or exportation is "consistent with the public interest." An exception is made for countries with which the United States has signed a free trade agreement (FTA), under which a public interest test is not required. The Federal Energy Regulatory Commission (FERC) must also approve the LNG terminal itself, and is charged with assessing and mitigating any environmental or public safety concerns posed by terminal construction or operation.

As of fall 2013, 25 companies had applied to the DOE for permission to export LNG (table 8.1). The majority of these applications have been approved for FTA countries. Yet of the 20 countries with which the United States has an FTA, only five—Korea, Mexico, Canada, Chile, and the Dominican Republic—currently import LNG, with Korea accounting for more than 90 percent of the total (International Gas Union 2012). Korea's 4.5 Bcfd import market is relatively large, but not nearly enough to absorb the 35 Bcfd of export applications before the DOE as of September 2013. Therefore, most companies also have applied for permission to export to non-FTA countries. The DOE approved one of Cheniere's Sabine Pass applications, but then put the others on hold pending a programmatic review of the effect of LNG exports on the domestic energy market and US economy. This review included two studies. The first, conducted by the EIA, examined the domestic energy market effects (EIA 2012d). The second, commissioned by an outside research company called NERA Economic Consulting, explored the macroeconomic effects (NERA 2012). Following publication of the NERA study, the DOE began a 75-day comment period, after which it began to act on the non-FTA applications in the queue.[2] As of September 2013, the DOE had approved three additional applications.

---

1. See United States Code Title 15, Section 717b.

2. Energy.gov, Office of Fossil Energy, LNG Export Study, available at www.fossil.energy.gov/programs/gasregulation/LNGStudy.html (accessed on September 8, 2013).

Table 8.1 Liquefied natural gas (LNG) export applications, 2012

Company	Location	Quantity (billion cubic feet per day)	DOE FTA approval	DOE non-FTA approval	FERC status
Sabine Pass Liquefaction (Cheniere)	Sabine Pass, TX	2.200	Approved	Approved	Certified
Freeport LNG Expansion/FLNG Liquefaction	Freeport, TX	1.400	Approved	Approved	Filed
Lake Charles Exports (Southern Union)	Lake Charles, LA	2.000	Approved	Approved	Filed
Dominion Cove Point LNG	Cove Point, MD	1.000	Approved	Approved	Filed
Jordan Cove Energy Project	Coos Bay, OR	1.200	Approved	Under review	Filed
Cameron LNG, LLC (Sempra)	Hackberry, LA	1.700	Approved	Under review	Filed
Freeport LNG Expansion/FLNG Liquefaction	Freeport, TX	1.400	Approved	Under review	Filed
Cheniere Marketing	Corpus Christi, TX	2.100	Approved	Under review	Filed
Oregon LNG	Astoria, OR	1.250	Approved	Under review	Filed
Golden Pass Products (ExxonMobil)	Sabine Pass, TX	2.600	Approved	Under review	Prefiled
Southern LNG Company (El Paso)	Elba Island, GA	0.500	Approved	Under review	Prefiled
Excelerate Liquefaction Solutions	Lavaca Bay, TX	1.380	Approved	Under review	Prefiled
CE FLNG (Cambridge Energy)	Plaquemines Parish, LA	1.070	Approved	Under review	Prefiled
Carib Energy	Various	0.030	Approved	Under review	Not filed
Main Pass Energy Hub, LLC	Offshore, LA	3.220	Approved	Under review	Not filed
Pangea LNG Holdings	Ingleside, TX	1.090	Approved	Under review	Not filed
Waller LNG Services	Cameron Parish, LA	0.160	Approved	Under review	Not filed
Sabine Pass Liquefaction (Cheniere)	Sabine Pass, TX	0.280	Approved	Under review	Not filed
Sabine Pass Liquefaction (Cheniere)	Sabine Pass, TX	0.240	Approved	Under review	Not filed
Gulf Coast LNG Export	Brownsville, TX	2.870	Approved	Under review	Not filed
Gulf LNG Liquefaction Company	Pascagoula, MS	1.500	Approved	Under review	Not filed
SB Power Solutions	Various	0.070	Approved	Not filed	Not filed
Magnolia LNG	Lake Charles, LA	0.540	Approved	Not filed	Prefiled
Gasfin Development, LLC	Cameron Parish, LA	0.200	Approved	Not filed	Not filed
Venture Global LNG, LLC	Various	0.670	Pending	Under review	Not filed
Eos LNG LLC	Brownsville, TX	1.600	Pending	Under review	Not filed
Barca LNG LLC	Brownsville, TX	1.600	Pending	Under review	Not filed
Sabine Pass Liquefaction (Cheniere)	Sabine Pass, TX	0.860	Pending	Under review	Not filed
Advanced Energy Solutions, LLC	Marin County, FL	0.020	Pending	Not filed	Not filed
Argent Marine Management, Inc.	Trussville, AL	0.003	Pending	Not filed	Not filed

FTA = free trade agreement

Sources: Department of Energy (DOE); Federal Energy Regulatory Commission (FERC).

Viability of US LNG Exports

Selling US natural gas abroad will generate export revenue, create jobs in the construction and operation of LNG terminals, and increase domestic production, with the attendant economic benefits described in chapter 4. At the same time, integrating US gas supply into the international gas market could increase domestic gas prices. Some policymakers and industry groups are concerned this will undermine the recent shale-boom-delivered increase in competitiveness of US energy-intensive manufacturing.[3]

The effect of LNG exports on domestic natural gas prices depends on the quantity exported, and exports face commercial as well as regulatory uncertainty. The number of export applications filed with the DOE is a poor indicator of the quantity of LNG the United States could commercially export. Total global LNG export capacity in 2012 totaled 38 Bcfd (IEA 2013b). Thus the 35 Bcfd of export capacity either already approved or under DOE review is likely more than the global LNG market could absorb. An additional 13.1 Bcfd of LNG export capacity is currently under construction (table 8.2), only 2.2 Bcfd of which is occurring in the United States (Sabine Pass). Another 56 Bcfd of capacity has been proposed outside of the United States. If all the projects currently proposed or under construction went ahead, there would be 139 Bcfd of global LNG export capacity, far in excess of the 55 Bcfd of LNG demand the IEA projects by 2035 (IEA 2012a). And given the multibillion-dollar investment required to construct an LNG export terminal—far more expensive than an import terminal—it is safe to say that much of the currently proposed global capacity ultimately will not be built.

It is in prospective LNG exporters' interests to file an application with the DOE, even if they are unsure about the commercial benefits of building a terminal. It costs only $50 to file an application, and given the uncertainty surrounding the DOE approval process for non-FTA countries, it makes sense to hold a place in the queue in the event the applications are decided on a first-come, first-serve basis. Filing a FERC application is a much more expensive process and signals a greater level of commitment. A company must perform preliminary front-end engineering design work with an engineering, procurement, and construction firm, as well as conduct extension emissions and hazardous materials modeling to comply with Environmental Protection Agency (EPA), Department of Transportation, and state regulations. Cheniere estimates that the FERC filing process cost more than $100 million and lasted 22 months. Outside of their Sabine Pass terminal, which has received FERC approval, eight others had been filed with FERC as of September 2013 (table 8.1), accounting for a combined 14 Bcfd (40 percent) of the 35 Bcfd either already approved or still in the DOE export queue. Many of the companies that have filed export applications with the DOE have yet to enter even the relatively inexpensive prefiling process with FERC.

---

3. Amy Harder, "Democratic Gas Blockade," *National Journal*, July 18, 2012.

Table 8.2 Global liquefied natural gas project landscape (billion cubic feet per day of export capacity)

Region	Operating	Under construction	Proposed
North America	0.0	2.2	37.3
United States	0.0	2.2	32.6
Canada	0.0	0.0	4.7
Latin America	2.6	0.0	2.5
Brazil	0.0	0.0	0.5
Colombia	0.0	0.0	0.1
Peru	0.6	0.0	0.0
Trinidad and Tobago	2.0	0.0	0.1
Venezuela	0.0	0.0	1.8
Europe	0.6	0.0	0.7
Cyprus	0.0	0.0	0.7
Norway	0.6	0.0	0.0
Eurasia	1.3	0.0	10.3
Russia	1.3	0.0	10.3
Middle East	13.2	0.0	10.4
Abu Dhabi	0.8	0.0	0.0
Iran	0.0	0.0	8.0
Iraq	0.0	0.0	0.6
Israel	0.0	0.0	0.3
Oman	1.5	0.0	0.0
Qatar	10.2	0.0	1.5
Yemen	0.9	0.0	0.0
Africa	8.2	1.3	13.2
Algeria	3.2	0.6	0.0
Angola	0.0	0.7	0.7
Cameroon	0.0	0.0	0.5
Egypt	1.5	0.0	0.5
Equatorial Guinea	0.5	0.0	0.6
Libya	0.1	0.0	0.8
Mozambique	0.0	0.0	1.4
Nigeria	2.9	0.0	8.0
Tanzania	0.0	0.0	0.9
Asia	11.8	9.7	14.0
Australia	3.2	8.0	10.1
Brunei	1.0	0.0	1.4
Indonesia	4.4	0.3	0.0
Malaysia	3.2	0.5	0.5
Papua New Guinea	0.0	0.9	2.1
Total	37.7	13.1	88.5

Sources: IEA (2012b); Department of Energy; Federal Energy Regulatory Commission; authors' estimates.

A number of consulting firms, university research institutes, and government forecasters have begun estimating how much LNG the United States could competitively export if given the green light from regulators. The International Energy Agency (IEA) has forecast roughly 4 Bcfd of combined US and Canadian LNG export by 2035, as they see Qatar, Australia, and others as better able to compete for future LNG demand (IEA 2012a). Navigant Consulting anticipates 4.8 Bcfd of US LNG exports by 2020 (Pickering 2012). Citigroup sees as much as 8 Bcfd of US exports by 2020 (Yuen et al. 2012), while researchers at Rice University's Baker Institute believe that "the next three decades do not indicate a future in which exports from the US Gulf Coast are profitable in the long term, at least not if developers are seeking a competitive rate of return to capital" (Medlock 2012).

The macroeconomic analysis commissioned from NERA by the DOE modeled a number of domestic supply and global LNG demand scenarios (NERA 2012). In their reference scenario, which is keyed to the EIA's 2011 study of US supply and demand and the IEA's figures for non-US supply and demand, the United States is unable to compete in international markets and thus does not export any LNG. In their demand-shock scenario, in which all Japanese nuclear power plants are shut down and replaced with natural gas, the United States exports 2.7 Bcfd in 2020 and 3.8 Bcfd by 2035. In their supply-demand shock scenario, in which both Japan and Korea move from nuclear to natural gas and no new LNG export capacity is built in Africa, Australia, or Southeast Asia, the United States exports 8 Bcfd in 2020 and 15.8 Bcfd by 2035. Under a high domestic US shale supply scenario, the United States exports 8.1 Bcfd of LNG in 2020 and 9.3 Bcfd by 2035, absent an international demand or supply shock. The demand shock scenario increases exports to 10.8 Bcfd and 15.4 Bcfd of exports by 2020 and 2035, respectively. In the supply-demand shock scenario, exports grow to 23 Bcfd by 2035.

A 2013 study by Charles River Associates takes issue with NERA's conservative export projections (Ditzel, Plewes, and Broxson 2013). They expect much more favorable economics for US LNG and expect the United States to export between 9 and 20 Bcfd by 2025 and between 20 and 35 Bcfd by 2030. This study remains an outlier among recent academic and industry projections.

Economic Impact

Studies analyzing the effect of LNG exports on domestic natural gas prices have largely focused on a range of 6 to 12 Bcfd. The 2011 EIA study commissioned by the DOE modeled both 6 Bcfd and 12 Bcfd under reference domestic gas assumptions, low shale gas estimated ultimate recovery (EUR) and high shale gas EUR scenarios. The EIA looked at the effects of both sudden and phased introductions of exports and found average domestic price increases between 2015 and 2035 of 1.3 to 1.8 percent per Bcfd of LNG exports (table 8.3). The NERA study was calibrated to the EIA's modeling results. Private sector estimates vary widely, from 0.6 percent per Bcfd in a 2011 Deloitte

Table 8.3   Natural gas price impact of US liquefied natural gas exports

Organization	Scenario	Export quantity (Bcfd)	Change in Henry Hub prices (percent)	Change per Bcfd (percent)
EIA reference	Low/slow	6.00	9.5	1.6
	Low/rapid	6.00	10.3	1.7
	High/slow	12.00	18.1	1.5
	High/rapid	12.00	21.0	1.7
EIA low shale EUR	Low/slow	6.00	9.4	1.6
	Low/rapid	6.00	10.6	1.8
	High/slow	12.00	18.2	1.5
	High/rapid	12.00	20.3	1.7
EIA high shale EUR	Low/slow	6.00	8.6	1.4
	Low/rapid	6.00	10.4	1.7
	High/slow	12.00	16.1	1.3
	High/rapid	12.00	21.8	1.8
Deloitte	n.a.	6.00	3.5	0.6
Navigant Consulting	n.a.	6.60	6.0	0.9
ICF International	n.a.	6.00	11.0	1.8
RBAC	1.0 Bcfd	1.00	2.9	2.9
	2.0 Bcfd	2.00	7.2	3.6
	4.0 Bcfd	4.00	16.9	4.2
	6.0 Bcfd	6.00	30.0	5.0
Charles River Associates	Likely export	20.00	22.2	1.1
	High export	35.00	43.1	1.2

n.a. = not available; Bcfd = billion cubic feet per day; EIA = Energy Information Administration; EUR = estimated ultimate recovery

Sources: EIA (2012d); Deloitte Center for Energy Solutions (2011); Ebinger, Massy, and Avasarala (2012); Brooks (2012); Ditzel, Plewes, and Broxson (2013).

study (Deloitte Center for Energy Solutions 2011) to 5 percent in an analysis by consultancy RBAC (Brooks 2012). These differences are attributable to the quantity of exports studied, assumptions about the price elasticity of demand for natural gas in US industry and power generation, and—most important— assumptions about the cost and supply of domestic natural gas.

With the exception of the RBAC study, a significant outlier, the price effects listed in table 8.3 are relatively modest at 6 Bcfd of exports. Even a 1.8 percent per Bcfd price increase (the upper-bound non-RBAC estimates and the average reference case increase of the studies listed in table 8.3 including RBAC) would translate into a 52 cent per MMBtu increase in Henry Hub gas prices relative to the average 2015–35 levels in EIA's 2013 natural gas price projections at 6 Bcfd of exports, and $1.04 per MMBtu at 12 Bcfd (EIA 2012b). That would modestly affect the international competitiveness of certain energy-intensive industries, such as petrochemicals, but would erode only part of the $2 per MMBtu and $4.3 per MMBtu decline in Henry Hub prices between 2015 and 2035 in our conservative and optimistic scenarios attributable to the shale gas boom. And as discussed in chapter 6, the share of US manufacturing for which low natural gas prices deliver a meaningful reduction in overall production costs is relatively small. If, however, the United States were to export 20 to 35 Bcfd of LNG, as the Charles River Associates report suggest, the effect on domestic natural gas prices would be more substantial, both for energy-intensive manufacturing and for residential and commercial consumers.

The NERA study models the negative effect of higher natural gas prices on US industrial output and household energy bills, as well as the positive effect on natural gas producer revenue and US terms of trade. It finds a very small net benefit to the US economy of exporting natural gas when there is sufficient commercial incentive to do so. This is consistent with two recent studies from the Brookings Institution (Levi 2012b; Ebinger, Massy, and Avasarala 2012). In NERA's supply-demand shock scenario, where exports increase to 8 Bcfd in 2020 and 15.8 Bcfd in 2035, US economic welfare improves by 0.029 percent. The NERA study finds that the macroeconomic benefits are greater as export quantities rise. There are important distributional effects of LNG exports—labor income declines while natural gas producer revenue increases—but on the whole the economy does better, albeit by a very small amount.

A number of industry groups criticized the NERA study following its release, claiming the study underestimates the economic benefits of using natural gas for domestic industry instead of export.[4] The Charles River Associates study also takes issue with NERA's findings, arguing that the economic value added and employment benefits of using 5 Bcfd of natural gas in manufacturing is greater than exporting 5 Bcfd as LNG. It does not, however, assess the effect of LNG exports on overall domestic production and thus does not estimate the extent to which LNG exports would ultimately come at the expense of supply to industry. As such, an apples-to-apples comparison with the NERA study is impossible. Just as the economic benefits of exporting LNG in the NERA study are quite small in the context of the economy as a whole, the macroeconomic effect of using that same gas for domestic manufacturing would also be quite small, as discussed in chapter 6.

One area where chemicals and LNG exports compete is in the market for engineering, procurement, and construction. Building a new petrochemical complex and building a new LNG export terminal are both multibillion dollar endeavors. Along the Gulf of Mexico, where construction of both is likely to be focused, competition for engineering and construction companies and labor could drive up engineering, procurement, and construction costs. This is what the Dutch disease literature suggests is likely to occur following a resource boom, and it may well pose a more significant challenge to the competitiveness of chemicals and other energy-intensive manufacturing than the effect of LNG exports on domestic energy prices.

---

4. Industrial Energy Consumers of America, "IECA Comments on Release of the DOE Study on LNG Exports," press release, December 5, 2012, www.ieca-us.com/wp-content/uploads/12.05.12_DOE-LNG-Export-Study-Press-Release.pdf (accessed on September 8, 2013).

Neither the NERA nor Charles River Associates studies quantify the economic effect of US natural exports on international LNG consumers and the knock-on benefits for the United States. Introducing Henry Hub–indexed US LNG exports, even in relatively modest quantities, could reduce the rents captured by traditional oil-linked LNG suppliers such as Qatar and Australia (Yuen et al. 2012; IEA 2012a, 2012b). It appears this has already occurred, before the first shipment of US LNG has hit the water. The prospect of US LNG exports has increased consumer negotiating leverage, with a Japanese utility signing a Henry Hub–linked contract with BP Singapore in late 2012.[5] All else equal, a more competitive global LNG market improves the global economic outlook and thus demand for other US goods and services. To the extent that US LNG exports allow Japanese and other utilities to reduce their consumption of crude oil, gasoline prices could be marginally lower for US drivers as well, which would yield additional economic benefits. Assessing the global effect of US LNG exports and implications for the US economy is analytically challenging, but an important area of study that has yet to be addressed.

Environmental Implications

Fear of higher natural gas prices is not the only source of opposition to proposed LNG export terminals. A number of environmental groups are worried about the potential effect on water and air quality as well as global climate change. Like all large industrial operations, LNG terminals can lead to local air and water pollution if not properly designed and managed. In addition, LNG terminals are a meaningful source of fugitive methane emissions, which, as discussed in chapter 7, are an important factor in global climate change. FERC seeks to ensure that terminals are designed to mitigate these environmental costs, which is part of why the filing process is so costly and time intensive.

Thus far, however, FERC has declined to assess the upstream environmental effect of LNG export terminals. This includes the fracking-related environmental issues discussed in chapter 7, which could become more pronounced if LNG exports significantly expand domestic natural gas production. In authorizing Cheniere's Sabine Pass terminal, FERC stated that "an overall increase in nationwide production of shale gas may occur for a variety of reasons, but the location and subsequent production activity is unknown, and too speculative to assume."[6] The Sierra Club has pushed back, claiming that the same modeling tools used for the EIA and NERA studies can be used to assess the effect of LNG exports on domestic shale gas supply, and that such an assessment is called for under the National Environmental Policy Act. The

---

5. Emiko Terazono, "Japan's LNG in Crucial Pricing Shift," *Financial Times*, December 18, 2012, www.ft.com/cms/s/0/a47a6efa-490e-11e2-b94d-00144feab49a.html?ftcamp=published_links/ rss/companies_energy/feed//product#axzz2Gqf0krw0 (accessed on September 8, 2013).

6. Hannah Mandel and Jenny Northey, "EPA Backs Sierra Club on LNG Export Review," *EnergyWire*, December 13, 2012, www.eenews.net/energywire/2012/12/13/2 (accessed on September 8, 2013).

Sierra Club and other environmental groups are also concerned that higher domestic natural gas prices due to US LNG exports could prompt US power generators to move back toward coal (Segall 2012). The EIA study found that 12 Bcfd of LNG exports could increase US CO_2 emissions by between 17 and 79 million tons per year, on average, between 2015 and 2035. That LNG would be consumed somewhere, and since climate change is a global problem, it is important to assess the non-US emissions effects of US natural gas exports. As with the global economic implications of US LNG exports, the global environmental implications are not yet well understood and deserve in-depth analysis.

Crude Oil

While the question of whether or not to export LNG is the most prominent trade policy debate prompted by the US oil and gas boom, others are waiting in the wings. The decline in US oil demand described in chapter 5—the result of weak economic growth, high oil prices, and increased fuel efficiency—has turned the United States into a net exporter of refined petroleum products. The United States exported more than 1 million bbl/d of refined products on net in 2012 versus net imports of 2 million bbl/d in 2007. This has led some policymakers to call for export restrictions to ensure that US oil is kept in the country (Nerurkar 2012). The president has the authority to restrict refined petroleum product exports under the Export Administration Act of 1979 but has not since 1981.[7]

Exporting crude oil, however, is currently prohibited in the United States without explicit presidential permission. Under the Mineral Leasing Act of 1920, to export domestically produced crude oil, the president must "make and publish an express finding that such exports will not diminish the total quantity or quality of petroleum available to the United States, and are in the national interest and are in accord with the provisions of the Export Administration Act of 1979."[8] The president must submit a report to Congress outlining the justification for any export permit, and Congress has 60 days to block the president's decision through a concurrent resolution. The Outer Continental Shelf Lands Act similarly restricts offshore oil production.[9] Past presidents have determined that the export of heavy Californian crude, crude produced from Alaska's Cook Inlet, and crude released from the Strategic Petroleum Reserve (SPR) are in the national interest (Nerurkar 2012). Congress has approved the exportation of oil shipped through the Trans-Alaska Pipeline, and under the North American Free Trade Agreement (NAFTA) crude exports to Canada are permitted, provided the crude is consumed within Canada and not reexported.

---

7. The one exception is petroleum products refined from Naval Petroleum Reserve crude oil, where an export license is required.

8. 30 United States Code 185(u).

9. 43 United States Code 1354.

Table 8.4　US refining capacity, 2011

Region	Nelson complexity index	Sulfur content (percent)	API gravity (degrees)	Capacity (operable, thousand barrels/day)	Production (gross input, thousand barrels/day)	Utilization rate (percent)
PADD I (East Coast)	8.9	0.71	33.09	1,618	1,100	68.0
PADD II (Midwest)	9.6	1.34	33.24	3,721	3,395	91.2
PADD III (Gulf Coast)	12.1	1.54	30.00	8,646	7,686	88.9
PADD IV (Rocky Mountains)	8.5	1.37	33.19	624	546	87.5
PADD V (West Coast)	10.7	1.35	27.59	3,117	2,561	82.2
US total	11.0	1.40	30.69	17,726	15,289	86.3

API = American Petroleum Institute; PADD = Petroleum Administration for Defense District

Sources: EIA (2011b); Oil & Gas Journal (2011).

While the United States exported 1 million bbl/d of refined products on net in 2012, it imported 8.4 million bbl/d of crude oil. That is a decline from 10 million bbl/d in 2007. In our optimistic scenario, net crude imports fall below 5 million bbl/d by 2020. Market developments may butt up against the export ban well before the United States becomes a net crude exporter, should that ultimately occur. US oil companies have invested considerable sums of money constructing world-class refineries that can process the heavier, higher-sulfur (also called sour) crude produced in Venezuela and the Middle East. The average US refinery has a Nelson complexity index[10] of 11 (table 8.4), compared with the non-US average of 6.1 (Oil & Gas Journal 2011). This is particularly true along the Gulf of Mexico—known in the industry as Petroleum Administration for Defense District III (PADD III)—home to half of US refining capacity. PADD III refineries are among the most sophisticated in the world, with a Nelson complexity index of 12.1 (table 8.4), and are among the best suited to process heavy, high-sulfur crudes.[11]

The problem is that the oil being produced from shale formations in North Dakota, Texas, New Mexico, and other parts of the US midcontinent is light and low-sulfur (also called sweet). While the refineries in PADD II (the Midwest) and PADD IV (the Rocky Mountains) are less complex than those in PADD III, together they have only half the capacity of PADD III refineries and are operating at very high utilization rates. There are some plans to expand existing midcontinent refineries, and even build a couple of new ones, but total additional US refining capacity currently in the works is only 100,000 bbl/d, less than one-fifth of current North Dakotan production (Murti, Carter-Tracy, and

---

10. The Nelson complexity index is a measure of how sophisticated a refinery is. For more information, see www.eia.gov/todayinenergy/detail.cfm?id=8330.

11. The weight of a crude oil is generally measured by API (American Petroleum Institute) gravity. Heavier crudes have a lower API gravity, while lighter crudes have a higher gravity. Sour crudes are those with a high sulfur content, while sweet crudes have a low sulfur content.

Kwon 2012). From a commercial standpoint, it may make sense to export light and sweet US production to refineries elsewhere in the world and continue to import heavy sour crudes to take advantage of existing Gulf of Mexico refinery investments. The question is whether policymakers will allow that kind of swap to occur given existing crude oil export restrictions and politicians' fascination with the concept of energy independence.

While export restrictions are not yet a meaningful limit on commercially efficient allocation of domestic crude oil supply, infrastructure constraints are, and they provide insight into the future tradeoffs of the US crude oil export ban. The US crude oil pipeline network was built to bring imported oil from the Gulf of Mexico to refineries in the country's interior. With declining domestic oil demand and surging domestic supply, midcontinent refineries have all the crude they need and producers are looking for ways to ship crude to refineries along the Gulf of Mexico or the East Coast. A shortage of pipelines, or at least pipelines headed in the right direction, has forced producers in North Dakota and elsewhere to rely on more expensive transportation options, such as rail and truck. In 2012, transportation bottlenecks meant that Bakken oil sold for $17 per barrel less on average than similar-quality crudes produced offshore in the Gulf of Mexico.[12] This has been great for midcontinent refiners, who have benefited from lower feedstock costs (figure 8.2). But little of that cost savings has been passed onto consumers, with midcontinent drivers paying roughly as much as their counterparts on the East Coast (figure 8.3). East Coast refineries, which rely on much more expensive sweet light crude, have been under tremendous pressure from their midcontinent competitors, with utilization rates dropping to 68 percent in 2011 (table 8.4). The situation improved in 2012 as East Coast refineries began sourcing large quantities of Bakken crude by rail.

Over the coming decade, new pipeline investments will likely close the current regional disparities in crude oil prices, but they could also put the US export ban to its first real test in several decades. The domestic rail system has proved surprisingly flexible and capable of moving crude oil from the Bakken to the East Coast; it is tough to compete with the economics of pipeline shipment to the Gulf. Yet while there is sufficient refining capacity in PADD III to absorb projected increases in midcontinent production, doing so at the expense of Middle East or other heavy sour crudes could potentially decrease global oil supply. Complex refineries, such as those in PADD III, can process light sweet oil as well as heavy sour crudes, though doing so incurs a commercial penalty because they are forced to idle expensive equipment used specifically for heavy crude. When simple refineries process heavy crude, the product yield declines dramatically, and in places such as Europe, with tight air quality regulations, simple refineries without the appropriate desulfurization technology cannot process sour crudes at all. So if PADD III refineries switch to sweet

---

12. Bloomberg data, accessed using the Bloomberg Terminal on July 1, 2013. Louisiana light and sweet versus Bakken spot prices.

Figure 8.2   Refinery acquisition cost of crude oil, 2004–12

US dollars per barrel

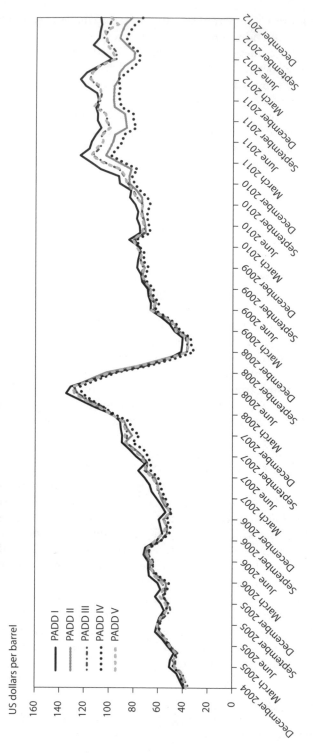

PADD = Petroleum Administration for Defense District

Source: EIA (2013a).

Figure 8.3 Wholesale gasoline prices, 2004–12

US dollars per gallon

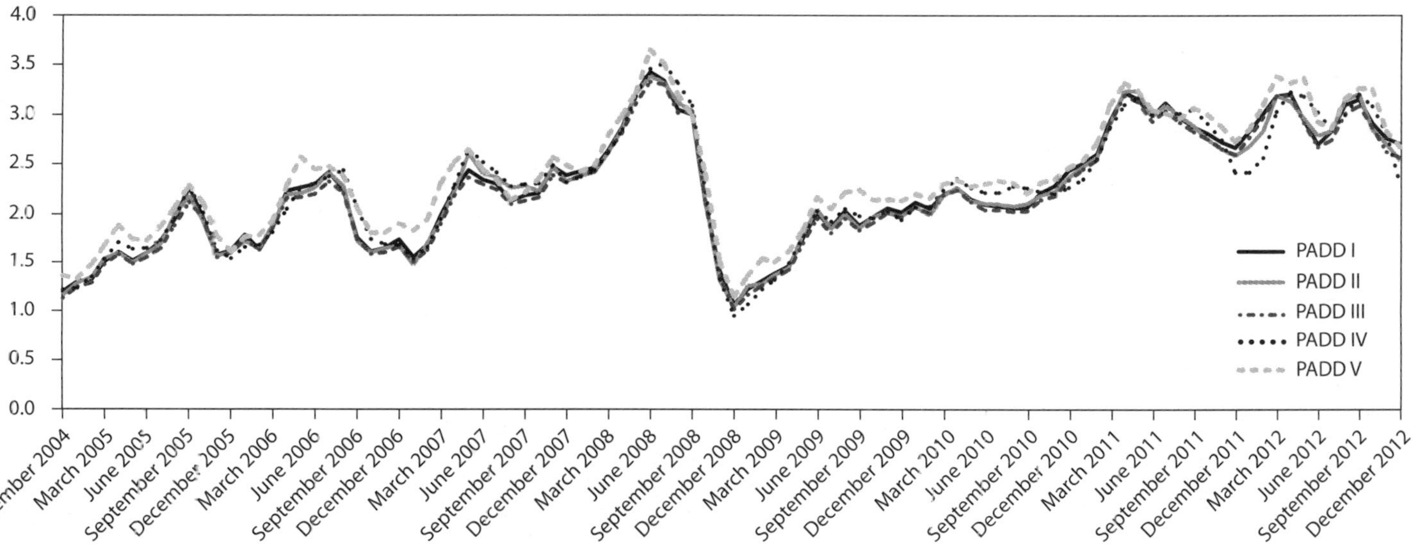

PADD I
PADD II
PADD III
PADD IV
PADD V

PADD = Petroleum Administration for Defense District

Source: EIA (2013a).

light domestic crudes, diverting heavy sour foreign crudes to simple refineries, total global production of gasoline, diesel, and other petroleum products could decline. If new complex refineries are built in other countries to handle redirected heavy sour supply, that investment will likely be recouped through higher gasoline and diesel prices. The refined product market is global, and there are no refined product import or export restrictions in the United States, so either of these developments would affect US consumers.

Shipping crude oil from the Gulf of Mexico to East Coast refineries could also be a commercially attractive alternative to refining it in PADD III or shipping it east by rail, but is complicated by the Merchant Marine Act of 1920—specifically Section 27 of that act, otherwise known as the Jones Act.[13] Under the Jones Act, all goods transported by water between two US ports must be transported on a ship built, owned, and operated by Americans. This requirement can be waived by the US Maritime Administration, which is part of the Department of Homeland Security, and it has been in instances of domestic fuel shortages that followed Hurricane Katrina in 2005 and Hurricane Sandy in 2012. But industry sources estimate that absent a waiver, the Jones Act raises the cost of shipping oil from the Gulf of Mexico to the Northeast by $3 to $4 per barrel.[14]

Given how rapidly the domestic oil supply and transportation infrastructure is evolving, it is difficult to say when and to what extent the crude oil export ban will start to meaningfully affect markets and what the implications will be for US consumers. But it is an important question, as this feature of US trade policy will receive more and more attention.

Coal

The US oil and gas boom is raising new trade policy issues directly through current LNG and looming crude export policy debates. But it indirectly raises another energy trade question: Should the United States export domestically produced coal? The country has long been a major coal producer, accounting for roughly one-quarter of global production over the past three decades and more than one-quarter of global proven reserves (BP 2013). Nearly 95 percent of this production has been for domestic use, as coal has fueled more than 50 percent of power generation and accounted for more than 20 percent of overall US energy supply since the early 1980s.

As discussed in chapter 7, however, coal's domestic market prospects have recently declined, hit first by the financial crisis and then by competition from low-cost shale gas. At the same time, coal demand outside the United States has remained relatively strong thanks to robust growth in emerging Asia. As a

---

13. Public Law 66-261.

14. John Bussey, "Oil and the Ghost of 1920," *Wall Street Journal*, September 13, 2012, http://professional.wsj.com/article/SB10000872396390444433504577649891243975440.html?mg=reno64-wsj (accessed on September 8, 2013).

Figure 8.4   Coal consumption and net exports, 2002–12

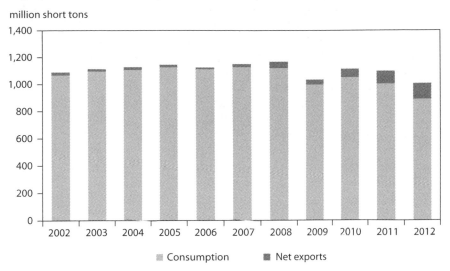

million short tons

Consumption   Net exports

Sources: EIA (2012b, 2013d).

result, US coal miners are increasingly turning to overseas markets to sell their product (figure 8.4). Net US coal exports soared between 2006 and 2012, from 13 million to 117 million short tons, and recently proposed coal infrastructure projects might increase US export capacity to more than 250 million short tons by 2020 and possibly as early as 2016.[15]

US coal exports have traditionally come primarily from the Appalachian region, given its close proximity to Eastern terminals that service the Atlantic Basin market. Much of the proposed export infrastructure, however, would give Western producers meaningful access to global markets for the first time, including rail lines and export terminals linking the giant Powder River Basin in Wyoming and Montana to the Asian seaborne coal market. Individually, these projects have attracted considerable attention in the communities where they are slated to be built, prompting vigorous debates about the local economic and environmental effects. Given the breadth and scale of current proposals and the fact that they would link the domestic coal market to global coal trade in new ways, there are important questions about their collective effects on national and regional energy markets and broader environmental quality as well. How will a significant increase in US coal exports affect the cost

---

15. Andy Blumenfeld, "Inland Rivers, Ports, and Terminals: Industry Outlook—Energy," PowerPoint presentation, St. Louis, MO, May 3, 2012. Blumenfeld is vice president of analysis and strategy at Arch Coal. Peabody's projections of US exports are slightly less aggressive than Arch's. According to a company presentation by Fred Palmer at the Argus America's Coal Summit in 2012, Peabody sees total US exports at 50 million to 170 million tons by 2020.

of coal in the United States? Given the current price disparity between Western coal and Chinese coal imports, how will linking the Powder River Basin to the Asian seaborne coal market change domestic US coal pricing? How will the power generation mix in the United States change and what will be the net effect on domestic air pollution? Perhaps most important, will exporting US coal displaced by domestic shale gas undermine recent CO_2 emission reductions the United States has achieved?

While coal exports have attracted considerable attention from the environmental community, there has been far less analysis of the potential economic and environmental effects than with LNG exports. This is partly because the federal government does not have as central a role in determining whether coal exports occur as it does with LNG. Most of the analysis of LNG exports was commissioned by either the federal government or outside groups looking to influence federal policy. The prospects for coal exports, on the other hand, depend much more on state and local policy surrounding individual export terminals, where national and international economic and environmental issues are not the primary focus. That said, the federal government does have a role in many of these projects, often through the Army Corps of Engineers, and the resulting National Environmental Policy Act review process could force Washington to grapple with some of the broader economic and environmental questions. Beyond the fate of any individual export terminal, the president has the power to block coal exports overall under the Export Administration Act of 1979, as with refined petroleum products.

Navigating the New Trade Policy Landscape

From a trade policy standpoint, the current oil and gas boom puts the United States in a challenging position. Washington has long led the charge against export restrictions in other countries, in the interest of protecting Americans' ability to access the imports, energy or otherwise, needed to keep the economy running. With domestic energy supply growing, US export restrictions that have been on the books for decades are starting to matter, forcing policymakers to reevaluate long-held trade policy beliefs. We are not lawyers and are not qualified to assess the legality of current or contemplated export restrictions in the United States. Our colleagues at the Peterson Institute for International Economics—Gary Clyde Hufbauer, Allie E. Bagnall, and Julia Muir—provide an excellent overview in a recent policy brief on LNG exports (Hufbauer, Bagnall, and Muir 2013). Drawing from their work, we briefly review the relevant provisions in international trade law and offer some principles for navigating this new energy trade policy landscape.

Oil, natural gas, and coal are all considered goods and thus subject to the disciplines of the General Agreement on Tariffs and Trade (GATT) and the World Trade Organization (WTO). Several GATT provisions are relevant to existing and contemplated US energy export restrictions. Article XI disciplines the use of nonfiscal export restrictions, such as quotas, export bans, or nonautomatic export licensing (Selivanova 2011). It states:

> No prohibition or restriction other than duties, taxes or other charges, whether made effective through quotas, import or export licenses or other measures, shall be instituted or maintained by any contracting party on the importation of any product of the territory or any other contracting party or on the exportation or sale for export of any product destined for the territory of any other party.

An allowance is made for "export prohibitions or restrictions temporarily applied to prevent or relieve critical shortages of foodstuffs or other products essential to the exportation of the contracting party." A country imposing an export restriction could also argue that the policy qualifies for one of the exceptions under Article XX, such as Article XX(g), which justifies measures "relating to the conservation of exhaustible natural resources." While natural gas, coal, and oil are all certainly exhaustible natural resources, to qualify for an Article XX(g) exception, US export restrictions would need to be coupled with "restrictions on domestic production or consumption." On the face of it, restrictions on American LNG exports would have a difficult time meeting this test, as the government is encouraging domestic natural gas production and consumption. Export restrictions on crude oil or coal could have a stronger case.

The United States could also argue for an Article XXI exception on national security grounds. This is the exception generally cited in defense of US short supply controls on crude oil and refined petroleum products and dual-use military items. Hufbauer, Bagnall, and Muir (2013) note that "while the short supply restrictions have never been challenged in the GATT or the WTO, they are suspect, especially since they are permanent, not temporary, as GATT Article XI(1) requires." Beyond the Article XI disciplines, US export restrictions could also come under the disciplines of the WTO's Agreement on Subsidies and Countervailing Measures if they result in a significant disconnect between domestic and international energy prices. Trading partners could accuse the United States of subsidizing domestic energy-intensive manufacturers at the expense of foreign competitors; indeed, that is the stated objective of many supporters of LNG export restrictions.

Analysis of the WTO consistency of existing and proposed US energy export restrictions will become increasingly important in the years ahead as the United States continues to move from being an energy importer to an energy exporter. Equally important, however, is asking first-order questions about how these restrictions affect broader US trade and foreign policy objectives. This starts with quantifying just how important they are to the US economy as a whole. In the case of LNG exports, while the potential effect on domestic natural gas prices might matter a great deal for parts of the chemicals industry, analysis suggests that the effect on the economy overall, whether positive or negative, will likely be small. This quantification is important because it allows policymakers to weigh the potential costs of retaliation.

The United States has pressed a number of countries to remove export restrictions in recent years, filing WTO cases against Canada over timber exports and against China over export of rare earth minerals and other raw materials. The United States argued forcefully for greater WTO disciplines on domestic energy price subsidies during the Doha Round of negotiations, and pressed Saudi Arabia to include commitments on natural gas price controls as part of its WTO accession agreement. The United States will continue to rely on international commodity markets for decades to come, and continue to have an interest in importing energy, food, and other natural resources from countries that might have or be considering export restrictions themselves. A number of large energy producers, including Russia, are currently negotiating their WTO accession agreements, and export restrictions or dual-pricing regimes are a topic of considerable debate.

Finally, policymakers should consider the effect of export restrictions on non–trade policy priorities. US diplomats are pressing their Japanese, Indian, and Chinese counterparts to reduce purchases of Iranian crude oil in a bid to force Tehran to abandon its nuclear weapons program. At the same time, US policymakers are debating whether it is in the US national interest to let these same countries import US natural gas. While US LNG isn't a real substitute for Iranian crude, the hypocrisy of a decision to prohibit non-FTA countries from buying US LNG would make Iran-related diplomacy more challenging.

9

Conclusion

The surprise turnaround in US oil and natural gas production is shaking up the global energy landscape. Public and private sector forecasters alike have significantly revised their US supply projections, and while considerable disagreement remains about the magnitude and duration of the boom, there is an emerging consensus that the recent surge in oil production will continue for at least another decade and the natural gas boom for the foreseeable future.

From an economic standpoint, the boom could not come at a better time. With unemployment still near 8 percent at the time of publication, a surge in oil and natural gas investment provides a welcome near-term economic boost, as does the resulting reduction in energy prices. The boom is like a stimulus package that combines tax cuts with infrastructure spending. We estimate the shale gas and tight oil revolution could increase annual GDP growth by as much as 0.2 percent on average between 2013 and 2020, boosting economic output by a cumulative 2.1 percent over that period. That is higher than the estimated effect of the American Recovery and Reinvestment Act between 2008 and 2013.

Over the long term, the economic impact is more modest. As the economy returns to full employment, general equilibrium effects start to kick in. Oil and gas will have to compete with other sectors for both labor and capital, with interest and wage rates rising as a result. As energy is a factor of production in and of itself, the boom in oil and gas supply increases long-term potential GDP by up to 1.4 percent, in our estimation. But this is a one-off change in level, rather than a sustained, productivity-driven improvement in annual economic growth. That makes it very different from the information technology (IT) revolution in the 1990s. It was not increased computer hardware and software output directly that made the IT revolution so economically important; it was the productivity improvements that hardware and software enabled in other sectors of the economy.

Energy has had such a transformative effect in the past. The development of coal as a substitute for wood enhanced overall economic productivity because coal was a more useful type of energy, more energy dense and thus more portable. The country was running out of trees in any event, so an alternative energy source was needed. Without coal, the US industrial revolution would not have been possible. Likewise, electricity is a far more useful form of energy than coal and its invention enabled a wide range of new industrial activities. With the current oil and gas boom, however, the country is not getting a new, more useful form of energy; it is getting the same kind of energy at a lower price. This is certainly economically helpful, as evidenced by the 1.4 percent increase in potential GDP mentioned above. It helps make the US economy less vulnerable to global oil price spikes, provided that vehicle and other energy efficiency improvements continue. But for the country as a whole, it is not transformative.

The oil and gas boom will, however, be far more important in the long-term economic outlooks of many states and industries than our nationwide estimates suggest. North Dakota has seen a faster drop in unemployment since the crisis than any state in the union, in large part because of the development of the Bakken shale formation. The North Dakota experience is replicable in other resource-rich states in the Great Plains and Rocky Mountains with small populations. Gulf Coast states stand to do well thanks to large-scale onshore and offshore development, the region's traditional role as headquarters to the US oil and gas industry, and new petrochemical investment. But in Pennsylvania and other Midatlantic or Midwestern states, oil and gas are still a relatively small share of overall employment and economic output.

Some industries will see a significant increase in demand for their products from oil and gas investment, or an increase in international competitiveness, thanks to low-cost natural gas. This is already visible in new investments in energy-intensive petrochemical facilities and plants manufacturing the steel pipe used in drilling operations. But any manufacturing renaissance resulting from the US oil and gas boom will be limited to a subset of the US manufacturing sector. Industries that could see a 5 percent or greater increase in output thanks to demand from new oil and gas investment account for only 6 percent of US manufacturing employment. Industries that could see their production costs fall by more than 2 percent thanks to low-cost natural gas account for only 5 percent of US manufacturing employment. The vast majority of US manufacturing is neither energy intensive nor specialized enough in products related to oil and gas investment to see much of an effect. For these industries, the net effect could even be negative if a decline in US energy imports results in real effective exchange rate appreciation, as resource-rich countries have experienced.

If the economic benefits of the oil and gas boom are not as great as its boosters claim, the environmental costs are not as dire as its critics warn. The local air and water pollution—and even earthquakes—that environmental and community groups fear will result from an increase in unconventional oil and gas development can be addressed through smart policy without significantly curtailing production. The United States successfully reduced the public health effects of steel manufacturing and electricity generation in the last century and can do the same for oil and gas today.

The increase in natural gas production has also yielded environmental benefits. Sulfur dioxide, NO_x, mercury, and CO_2 emissions have all fallen sharply in recent years, thanks in part to the substitution of natural gas for coal in US power generation. But the low-hanging fruit has been picked and low-cost natural gas alone is unlikely to deliver significant additional emission reductions. For that, new policy is required.

Following the failure of cap-and-trade legislation in the US Senate in 2009, many environmental groups have given up on climate policy and focused their efforts on trying to block investment in new sources of fossil fuel supply. Yet the unconventional oil and gas boom potentially makes climate policy—whether a carbon tax, a clean energy standard, or Environmental Protection Agency regulation—cheaper and more politically palatable. A modest carbon tax, for example, would actually increase revenue to fossil fuel producers while simultaneously reducing greenhouse gas emissions. And the United States would still see higher economic and employment growth and lower energy costs than in a future with limited unconventional oil and gas production.

Finally, the turnaround in US oil and gas supply and decline in US energy demand are rapidly changing the country's energy trade position. This raises trade policy questions that Americans have not had to consider for decades. If the United States exports natural gas, will it undermine US manufacturing's newfound energy cost advantage? If the current ban on crude oil exports is lifted, what does it mean for US energy security? What are the environmental consequences if US coal producers start selling abroad what they used to sell at home, thanks to a natural gas–driven reduction in domestic demand? These are important and complex questions, and for many, further research is needed. But there is no evidence yet that allowing open trade in US energy resources will undermine the domestic economic, environmental, or security benefits of the boom, or that obstructing trade carries significant risks to the broader US trade and economic policy agenda.

Appendix A
Modeling Framework
and Assumptions

Our analysis of the economic and environmental effects of the US oil and gas boom relies heavily on the RHG-NEMS model, a version of the Energy Information Administration's (EIA) National Energy Modeling System (NEMS) maintained by the Rhodium Group (RHG), a New York–based economic research firm. The EIA uses NEMS to produce its *Annual Energy Outlook* (AEO), which projects the production, conversion, consumption, trade, and price of energy in the United States through 2035. NEMS is an energy-economic model that combines a detailed representation of the US energy sector with a macro-economic model provided by IHS Global Insight. The version of RHG-NEMS used for this analysis is keyed to the 2012 version of the AEO. Complete NEMS documentation is available on the EIA's website at www.eia.gov/oiaf/aeo/overview/index.html. Documentation of the macroeconomic and energy sector assumptions used in the AEO 2012 version of NEMS is available at www.eia.gov/forecasts/archive/aeo12/index.cfm.

NEMS is designed as a modular system, with a module for each major source of energy supply, conversion activity, and demand sector, as well as the international energy market and the US economy. The integrating module acts as a control panel, executing other NEMS modules to ensure energy market equilibrium in each projection year. The solution methodology of the modeling system is based on the Gauss-Seidel algorithm. Under this approach, the model starts with an initial solution, energy quantities, and prices, and then iteratively goes through each of the activated modules to arrive at a new solution. That solution becomes the new starting point and the above process repeats itself. The cycle repeats until the new solution is within the user-defined range of the previous solution. Then the model is said to have converged, producing the final output.

Oil and Gas Supply Module

In NEMS, oil and gas production is estimated by the oil and gas supply module (OGSM). OGSM estimates both conventional and unconventional supply from six lower-48 onshore regions, three offshore regions, and Alaska.[1] The module relies on the forecasted profitability of current and new projects to determine drilling and well development activities, subject to government regulations and restrictions. To estimate profitability, the module uses a range of exogenous variables—resource levels, finding-rate parameters, costs, production profiles, and tax rates—as well as inputs from other modules, including natural gas production and wellhead prices provided by the natural gas transmission and distribution module (NGTDM), crude oil wellhead prices at the OGSM regional level from the petroleum market model (PMM), and economic variables—principally interest rates and GDP deflators—from the macroeconomic activity module (MAM). The primary outputs of the OGSM are natural gas supply curves, which the NGTDM uses to estimate natural gas production, and crude oil production, used by the PMM. Technically recoverable resources are defined exogenously based on estimates from the United States Geological Survey (USGS) and the Bureau of Ocean Energy Management (BOEM).[2]

Macroeconomic Activity Module (MAM)

The MAM not only provides economic inputs to other modules as mentioned above, but also estimates the effects of changes in energy prices and demand produced in other modules on a wide range of macroeconomic variables. The MAM comprises three discrete models:[3]

1. IHS Global Insight's model of the US economy,
2. IHS Global Insight's industrial output and employment by industry models, and
3. EIA's regional models.

IHS Global Insight's model of the US economy is the same model IHS Global Insight uses to produce its economic forecasts for the company's monthly assessment of the US economy. The IHS Global Insight US model used for AEO 2012 is the US2010C version. EIA's industrial output and employment by industry models are derivatives of IHS Global Insight's industrial output and employment by industry models. The models have been

---

1. NEMS OGSM documentation as archived for AEO 2011, www.eia.gov/FTPROOT/modeldoc/ m063(2011).pdf (accessed on September 8, 2013).

2. Details of the estimates used in AEO 2012 can be obtained in OGSM assumptions for AEO 2012, www.eia.gov/forecasts/aeo/assumptions/pdf/oil_gas.pdf (accessed on September 8, 2013).

3. Much of this description is pulled from the NEMS macroeconomic activity module documentation as archived for the AEO 2012, www.eia.gov/forecasts/nemsdoc/macroeconomic/pdf/m065 (2012).pdf (accessed on September 8, 2013).

tailored to provide the industrial output and employment by industry detail the NEMS requires. The EIA's regional models consist of models of economic activity, industrial output, employment by industry, and commercial floor space. The first two models were developed during 2004 for use in preparing AEO 2005. The regional models were reestimated for AEO 2010.

All of the MAM models are linked to provide a fully integrated approach to forecasting economic activity at the national, industrial, and regional levels. IHS Global Insight's model of the US economy determines the national economy's growth path and the final demand mix. The EIA's industrial output model ensures that supply by industry is consistent with the final demands (consumption, investment, government spending, exports and imports) forecasted in the US model. Industrial output is the key driver of the employment forecast in EIA's employment by industry model. The employment by industry forecast also incorporates aggregate hours per week and productivity trends forecasted in the US model. The employment by industry forecast is aligned with the aggregate employment forecast of the US model. Key inputs to the EIA's regional models include forecasts of national output and employment by industry, population, nation, income, and housing activity. The EIA's regional models then forecast levels of industrial output, employment by industry, population, incomes, and housing activity for each of the nine census divisions. The sum of each of these concepts across the nine census divisions is aligned with the national totals forecasted by the US model. Together, these models of the US economy, industrial output, employment by industry, and regional economic activity constitute the macroeconomic activity module of the National Energy Modeling System.

Before the MAM can execute its suite of models, though, it requires exogenous assumptions regarding energy prices, consumption, and domestic production. Over 70 energy prices and quantities are extracted from the output of the demand and supply modules of the NEMS. Transformations of the exogenous assumptions are necessary to map these inputs from the NEMS into more aggregated concepts in the MAM. After the appropriate transformations are done, the US, industrial output, employment by industry, and regional models execute in sequence to produce a forecast of economic activity at the national, industrial, and regional levels. Drawn from the forecast are economic driver variables that are then passed to the NEMS supply, demand, and conversion modules. The NEMS then reacts to the new economic activity assumptions.

Forecasts of energy prices and quantities based upon the new economic assumptions are then passed back to the MAM. A NEMS cycle is complete once all the modules of the NEMS solve. Cycles are repeated as the NEMS iterates to a stable solution. There are a few industrial output and employment by industry concepts for which forecasts in the MAM are determined by the NEMS. The MAM's forecast of industrial output for the five energy-related sectors is based on growth rates extracted from the appropriate modules in the NEMS. The growth rates in output of petroleum refining, coal mining, oil and gas extraction, electric utilities, and gas utilities are applied to the last historical value of the appropriate series in the MAM's industrial output model. A similar computation is done for employment by industry, but for only two of the five energy sectors. Growth in employment is computed for coal mining and for oil and gas extraction using forecasts from the appropriate NEMS modules. These growth rates are then applied to the last historical value of the appropriate series in the MAM's employment by industry model.

Econometric models built in the 1950s and 1960s were largely Keynesian income-expenditure systems that assumed a closed domestic economy. High computation costs involving statistical estimation and model manipulation, along with the underdeveloped state of macroeconomic theory, limited the size of the models and the richness of the linkages of spending to financial conditions, inflation, and international developments. Since that time, however, computer costs have fallen spectacularly. Macroeconomic theory also has benefited from five decades of postwar data observation and from the intellectual attention of many eminent economists.

An Econometric Dynamic Equilibrium Growth Model

IHS Global Insight's model of the US economy strives to incorporate the best insights of many theoretical approaches to the business cycle: Keynesian, neoclassical, monetarist, supply-side, and rational expectations. In addition, the model embodies the major properties of the long-term growth models presented by James Tobin, Robert Solow, Edmund Phelps, and others. This structure guarantees that short-run cyclical developments will converge to a robust long-run equilibrium.

In growth models, the expansion rates of technical progress, the labor force, and the capital stock—both physical capital and human capital—determine the productive potential of an economy. Both technical progress and the capital stock are governed by investment, which in turn must be in balance with post-tax capital costs, available savings, and the capacity requirements of current spending. As a result, monetary and fiscal policies will influence both the short- and long-term characteristics of such an economy through their effects on national saving and investment.

A modern model of output, prices, and financial conditions is melded with the growth model to present detailed, short-run dynamics of the economy. In specific goods markets, the interactions of a set of supply and demand relations determine spending, production, and price levels. Typically, the level of inflation-adjusted demand is driven by prices, income, wealth, expectations, and financial conditions. The capacity to supply goods and services is keyed to a production function combining the basic inputs of labor hours, energy usage, and the capital stocks of business equipment and structures and government infrastructure. The total factor productivity of this composite of tangible inputs is driven by expenditures on research and development that produce technological progress.

Prices adjust in response to short-run gaps between current production and supply potential and to changes in the cost of inputs. Wages adjust to labor supply-demand gaps (indicated by a demographically adjusted unemployment rate), current and expected inflation (with a unit long-run elasticity), productivity, tax rates, and minimum wage legislation. The supply of labor responds positively to the perceived availability of jobs, to the after-tax wage level, and to the growth and age-gender mix of the population. Demand for labor is keyed to the level of output in the economy and to the productivity of labor, capital, and energy. Because the capital stock does not change much in the short run, a higher level of output requires more employment and energy inputs. Such increases are not necessarily equal to the percentage increase in output because of the improved efficiencies typically achieved during an upturn. Tempering the whole process of wage and price determination is the exchange rate; a rise signals prospective losses of jobs and markets unless costs and prices are reduced.

For financial markets, the model predicts exchange rates, interest rates, stock prices, loans, and investments interactively with the preceding GDP and inflation variables. The Federal Reserve sets the supply of reserves in the banking system and the fractional reserve requirements for deposits. Private sector demands to hold deposits are driven by national income, expected inflation, and the deposit interest yield relative to the yields offered on alternative investments. Banks and other thrift institutions, in turn, set deposit yields based on the market yields of their investment opportunities with comparable maturities and on the intensity of their need to expand reserves to meet legal requirements. In other words, the contrast between the supply and demand for reserves sets the federal funds rate, the critical short-term interest rate for interbank transactions. Other interest rates are keyed to this rate, plus expected inflation, Treasury borrowing requirements, and sectoral credit demand intensities.

The old tradition in macroeconomic model simulations of exogenous fiscal policy changes was to hold the Federal Reserve's supply of reserves constant at baseline levels. While this approach makes static analysis easier in the classroom, it sometimes creates unrealistic policy analyses when a dynamic model is appropriate. In IHS Global Insight's model of the US economy, monetary policy is defined by a set of targets, instruments, and regular behavioral linkages between targets and instruments. The model user can choose to define unchanged monetary policy as unchanged reserves, or as an unchanged reaction function in which interest rates or reserves are changed in response to changes in such policy concerns as the price level and the unemployment rate.

Monetarist Aspects

The model pays due attention to valid lessons of monetarism by carefully representing the diverse portfolio aspects of money demand and capturing the central bank's role in long-term inflationary trends. The private sector may demand money balances as one portfolio choice among transactions media (currency, checkable deposits), investment media (bonds, stocks, short-term securities), and durable assets (homes, cars, equipment, structures). Given this range of choices, each asset's implicit and explicit yield must therefore match expected inflation, offset perceived risk, and respond to the scarcity of real savings. Money balances provide benefits by facilitating spending transactions and can be expected to rise almost proportionately with transactions requirements unless the yield of an alternative asset changes.

Now that even demand deposit yields can float to a limited extent in response to changes in Treasury bill rates, money demand no longer shifts quite as sharply when market rates change. Nevertheless, the velocity of circulation—the ratio of nominal spending to money demand—is still far from stable during a cycle of monetary expansion or contraction. Thus the simple monetarist link from money growth to price inflation or nominal spending is considered invalid as a rigid short-run proposition.

Equally important, as long-run growth models demonstrate, induced changes in capital formation can also invalidate a naïve long-run identity between monetary growth and price increases. Greater demand for physical capital investment can enhance the economy's supply potential in the event of more rapid money creation or new fiscal policies. If simultaneous, countervailing influences deny an expansion of the economy's real potential, the model will translate all money growth into a proportionate increase in prices rather than in physical output.

Supply-Side Economics

Since 1980, supply-side political economists have pointed out that the economy's growth potential is sensitive to the policy environment. They have focused on the potential labor supply, capital spending, and savings effects of tax rate changes. IHS Global Insight's model of the US economy embodies supply-side hypotheses to the extent supportable by empirical evidence in the available data. This is considerable in the many areas that supply-side hypotheses share with long-run growth models. These features, however, have been fundamental ingredients of the model since 1976.

Rational Expectations

As the rational expectations school has pointed out, much of economic decision making is forward looking. The decision to buy a car or a home is not only a question of current affordability but also one of timing. The delay of a purchase until interest rates or prices decline has become particularly common since the mid-1970s when both inflation and interest rates were very high and volatile. Consumer sentiment surveys, such as those conducted by the University of Michigan Survey Research Center, clearly confirm this speculative element in spending behavior. However, households can be shown to base their expectations, to a large extent, on their past experiences: They believe that the best guide to the future is an extrapolation of recent economic conditions and the changes in those conditions. Consumer sentiment about whether a certain time is a "good time to buy" can therefore be modeled as a function of recent levels and changes in employment, interest rates, inflation, and inflation expectations. Similarly, inflation expectations (influencing financial conditions) and market strength expectations (influencing inventory and capital spending decisions) can be modeled as functions of recent rates of increase in prices and spending.

A largely retrospective approach is not, of course, wholly satisfactory to pure adherents of the rational expectations doctrine. This group argues that the announcement of macroeconomic policy changes would significantly influence expectations of inflation or growth before any realized change in prices or spending. If an increase in government expenditures is announced, the argument purports, expectations of higher taxes to finance the spending might lead to lower consumer or business spending despite temporarily higher incomes from the initial government spending stimulus. A rational expectations theorist would thus argue that multiplier effects tend to be smaller and more short-lived than a mainstream economist would expect.

The rational expectations propositions are subject to empirical evaluation. IHS Global Insight's conclusions are that expectations play a significant role in private sector spending and investment decisions, but until change has occurred in the economy, there is very little room for significant changes in expectations of the variable about which the expectation is formed. The rational expectations school thus correctly emphasizes a previously understated element of decision making but exaggerates its significance for economic policymaking and model building.

IHS Global Insight's model of the US economy allows a choice in this matter. The user can simply accept IHS Global Insight's judgments and let the model translate policy initiatives into initial changes in the economy, simultaneous or delayed changes in expectations, and subsequent changes in the economy. Or the user can manipulate the clearly identified expectations variables in the model, that is, consumer sentiment and inflation expectations. If the user believes that fear of higher taxes would subdue spending, the user can reduce the consumer sentiment index.

Theory as a Constraint

The conceptual basis of each equation in IHS Global Insight's model of the US economy was thoroughly worked out before the regression analysis was initiated. The list of explanatory variables includes a carefully selected set of demographic and financial inputs. Each estimated coefficient was then thoroughly tested to be certain that it met the tests of modern theory and business practice. This attention to equation specification and coefficient results eliminated the short circuits that can occur in evaluating a derivative risk or an alternative policy scenario. Because each equation will stand up to a thorough inspection,

IHS Global Insight's model is a reliable analytical tool and can be used without excessive iterations. The model is not a black box: It functions like a personal computer spreadsheet, in which each interactive cell has a carefully computed, theoretically consistent entry and thus performs logical computations simultaneously.

Model Enhancements

We made one major enhancement to the MAM for our analysis. The MAM estimates upstream oil and gas investment based on energy prices passed to the MAM from other modules. Higher prices increase investment and lower prices decrease investment. This estimation technique works well in most cases since the price elasticity of oil supply is quite low and small changes in supply produce large changes in price (and vice versa). In our analysis, however, we are examining the effect of a large increase in the resource base (positive supply shock), which in the model leads to lower prices and thus lower investment in oil and gas—the opposite of what is actually occurring. We correct for this by estimating the increase in upstream oil and gas investment associated with our conservative and optimistic scenarios outside of NEMS and adjusting upstream oil and gas investment demand in the MAM accordingly. Our investment estimates are based on a 2012 IHS Global Insight study (IHS CERA 2012) that included detailed estimates of the investment required to produce unconventional oil and gas. We multiply IHS CERA's per barrel and per cubic foot oil and natural gas investment estimates by the difference in production among our pre-shale, conservative, and optimistic scenarios to estimate the additional investment required to achieve the production increases associated with each scenario. These investment estimates are calculated endogenously in the model and added to the baseline upstream oil and gas investment demand projections in the MAM. As the model converges, it captures the macroeconomic effect of this increase in investment demand, including higher demand for the goods and services needed to produce oil and gas, as well as increased competition for capital in other sectors thanks to higher interest rates.

Scenario Descriptions

We developed our three core scenarios—pre-shale, conservative, and optimistic—based on the version of NEMS used to produce AEO 2012. Unless modified for the purpose of the analysis, the assumptions across all three scenarios are calibrated to AEO 2012's reference case.[4] This case takes into account all current laws and regulations affecting the energy sector and assumes that such laws and regulations are unchanged through the projection period.

---

4. For further discussion of assumptions included in the reference case, refer to the *Annual Energy Outlook 2012*, www.eia.gov/forecasts/archive/aeo12/pdf/0383(2012).pdf (accessed on September 8, 2013).

Pre-Shale

This scenario acts as a baseline for our analysis and is intended to represent what the US energy market and economy would look like had the shale gas and tight oil boom not occurred. To do this, we changed model estimates for technically recoverable resources (TRR) of natural gas to 125 trillion cubic feet (tcf), the levels included in AEO 2008, as opposed to the 482 tcf levels included in the AEO 2012 reference case. Development of onshore unconventional oil resources, especially tight oil, between 2008 and 2012 led to an upward revision in EIA estimates for onshore unproven resources to 113 billion barrels in AEO 2012. In our pre-shale scenario, we lower unproven resources to 81 billion barrels, near AEO 2008 levels. Compared with the AEO 2012 reference case, estimated ultimate recovery (EUR) per tight oil well and shale gas well is assumed to be 75 and 50 percent lower, respectively. In addition, we assume that the moratorium on offshore development, which President George W. Bush lifted in 2008, is still in place. The AEO 2012 reference case assumes a constant 0.9 tcf of liquefied natural gas (LNG) exports from 2020 through 2035. Such exports are possible only due to the shale gas revolution. Hence in the pre-shale case, we assume no LNG exports.

Conservative

We use the AEO 2012 reference case for our conservative scenario, as its projections are near the bottom of recent supply forecasts, including the AEO 2013 early release. All assumptions are the same as the AEO 2012 reference case with the exception of upstream oil and gas investment in the MAM, where the investment patch described above is applied.

Optimistic

The optimistic case represents the upper end of recent oil and natural gas supply projections. The starting point of this scenario is the EIA's high TRR case from AEO 2012, wherein well spacing for all tight oil and shale gas plays is assumed to be 8 wells per square mile, EUR per tight oil and shale gas well is assumed to be 75 and 50 percent higher than the reference case, respectively, and total unproved onshore oil and shale gas TRR is increased to 184 billion barrels and 1,091 tcf, respectively. Offshore, we assume all currently unexplored regions, including the Atlantic and Pacific outer continental shelves, are available for leasing in 2013. Resource restrictions are relaxed to increase the maximum number of wells that can be developed each year. We increase exploration success rates to reflect greater exploration and development and reduce delays between exploration and development. Finally we revise offshore TRR estimates up by 1.5 times for the lower 48 and 3 times for Alaska compared with the reference case.

Corporate Average Fuel Economy (CAFE) Side Cases

Our core scenarios include joint attribute-based CAFE and vehicle greenhouse gas (GHG) emissions standards for model year (MY) 2012 to MY2016 light-duty vehicles (LDVs). In 2011 the Environmental Protection Agency (EPA) and National Highway Traffic Safety Administration (NHTSA) jointly announced the Heavy-Duty National Program, which for the first time establishes GHG emissions and fuel consumption standards for on-road heavy-duty trucks and their engines. Our core scenarios include these new standards for heavy-duty vehicles (HDVs), which begin for MY2014 vehicles and engines and are fully phased in by MY2018. To estimate the effect of CAFE standards in chapter 6, we model two side cases for each scenario. Our no-CAFE case keeps CAFE standards for LDVs at MY2011 levels and removes the HDV standards. Our full CAFE side case includes the HDV standards, the LDV MY2012–16 standards, and the recently adopted LDV standards for MY2017–25.

Carbon Price Side Cases

In the carbon price side cases, a carbon tax is applied across all sectors of the economy. The tax starts in 2013 at $15 per metric ton of CO_2 equivalent and increases at an inflation-adjusted rate of 5 percent per year throughout the projection period.[5] Since the Fukushima Daiichi nuclear disaster, there is increased opposition to building new nuclear power plants in the United States and around the world. To model this new constraint, we increase the nuclear power plant capital cost by 25 percent relative to the AEO 2012 reference case. This change is made in both the core scenarios and side cases but only has a material effect in the carbon price side cases.

---

5. The application of carbon tax mirrors AEO 2012's GHG15 side case. For details, see *Annual Energy Outlook 2012*, www.eia.gov/forecasts/archive/aeo12/pdf/0383(2012).pdf (accessed on September 8, 2013).

References

ACC (American Chemistry Council). 2011. *Shale Gas and New Petrochemicals Investment: Benefits for the Economy, Jobs, and US Manufacturing.* Washington.

Adkins, J. Marshall, and Pavel Molchanov. 2012. *Yes, Mr. President, We Believe We Can Drill Our Way Out of This Problem.* St. Petersburg, FL: Raymond James.

Aghion, Philippe, and Peter Howitt. 2009. *The Economics of Growth.* Cambridge, MA: MIT Press.

Allen, D. T., V. M. Torres, J. Thomas, D. W. Sullivan, M. Harrison, A. Hendler, and J. H. Seinfeld. 2013. Measurements of methane emissions at natural gas production sites in the United States. *Proceedings of the National Academy of Sciences.* Available at www.pnas.org/content/early/2013/09/10/1304880110.

Ayres, Robert U., and Benjamin Warr. 2005. Accounting for Growth: The Role of Physical Work. *Structural Change and Economic Dynamics* 16, no. 2 (June): 181–209.

Baker Hughes. 2012. Rig Data. Available at www.bakerhughes.com/rig-count.

BEA (Bureau of Economic Analysis). 2013. *National Income and Product Accounts.* Washington: US Department of Commerce.

Blanchard, Olivier J., and Jordi Gal. 2007. *The Macroeconomic Effects of Oil Price Shocks: Why Are the 2000s so Different from the 1970s?* NBER Working Paper 13368. Cambridge, MA: National Bureau of Economic Research.

BLS (Bureau of Labor Statistics). 2013a. *Current Employment Survey.* Washington.

BLS (Bureau of Labor Statistics). 2013b. *Quarterly Census of Employment and Wages.* Washington.

BLS (Bureau of Labor Statistics). 2013c. *Consumer Price Index.* Washington.

BLS (Bureau of Labor Statistics). 2013d. *Consumer Expenditure Survey.* Washington.

Bordoff, Jason. 2013. There Will Be Oil. *Democracy* 29, no. 13 (Summer).

BP (British Petroleum). 2006. *Statistical Review of World Energy 2006.* London: BP PLC.

BP (British Petroleum). 2008. *Statistical Review of World Energy 2008.* London: BP PLC.

BP (British Petroleum). 2012. *Statistical Review of World Energy 2012.* London: BP PLC.

BP (British Petroleum). 2013. *Energy Outlook 2030.* London: BP PLC.

Brackett, Bob. 2012. *For Halloween, a Chart that Could Scare the Oil Bulls*. New York: Bernstein Research.

Bradbury, James, Michael Obeiter, Laura Draucker, Wen Wang, and Amanda Stevens. 2013. *Clearing the Air: Reducing Upstream Greenhouse Gas Emissions from US Natural Gas Systems*. Washington: World Resources Institute.

Brooks, Robert. 2012. *Using GPCM® to Model LNG Exports from the US Gulf Coast*. RBAC Inc.

Carter, Susan B., Scott Sigmund Gartner, Michael R. Haines, Alan L. Olmstead, Richard Sutch, and Gavin Wright. 2006. *Historical Statistics of the United States Millennial Edition Online*, ed. Peter H. Lindert and Richard Sutch. New York: Cambridge University Press.

CBO (Congressional Budget Office). 2012. *Estimated Impact of the American Recovery and Reinvestment Act on Employment and Economic Output from April 2012 through June 2012*. Washington.

CBO (Congressional Budget Office). 2013. *The Budget and Economic Outlook: Fiscal Years 2013 to 2023*. Washington.

CEA (Council of Economic Advisers). 2013. *Economic Report of the President*. Washington: US Government Printing Office.

Census Bureau. 2012. *Annual Survey of Manufactures*. Washington: US Department of Commerce.

Cline, William R., and John Williamson. 2011. *Estimates of Fundamental Equilibrium Exchange Rates, May 2011*. Policy Brief 11-5. Washington: Peterson Institute for International Economics.

Collins, Christopher M., Mark C. Sadeghian, Gregory Fodell, and Sean T. Sexton. 2012. *Dark Side of the Boom*. Fitch Ratings. Available via subscription at www.fitchratings.com.

CMS (Centers for Medicare and Medicaid Services). 2011. *National Health Expenditures*. US Department of Health and Human Services.

Corden, W. M. 1984. Booming Sector and Dutch Disease Economics: Survey and Consolidation. *Oxford Economic Papers* 36, no. 3: 359–80.

Credit Suisse. 2011. *Triple Digit Oil, Raising Prices*. New York.

Deloitte Center for Energy Solutions. 2011. *Made in America: The Economic Impact of LNG Exports from the United States*. Available at www.deloitte.com/assets/Dcom-UnitedStates/Local%20Assets/Documents/Energy_us_er/us_er_MadeinAmerica_LNGPaper_122011.pdf.

Deutch, John, James R. Schlesinger, and David G. Victor. 2006. *National Security Consequences of U.S. Oil Dependency*. New York: Council of Foreign Relations.

Deutsche Bank. 2011. *US Fixed Income Weekly*. New York.

Ditzel, Ken, Jeff Plewes, and Bob Broxson. 2013. *US Manufacturing and LNG Exports: Economic Contributions to the US Economy and Impacts on US Natural Gas Prices*. Washington: Charles River Associates.

DOE (Department of Energy). 2009. *Modern Shale Gas Development in the United States: A Primer*. Washington.

Dynan, Karen E., Jonathan Skinner, and Stephen P. Zeldes. 2004. Do the Rich Save More? *Journal of Political Economy* 112, no. 2: 397–444.

Ebinger, Charles, Kevin Massy, and Govinda Avasarala. 2012. *Liquid Markets: Assessing the Case for US Exports of Liquefied Natural Gas*. Washington: Brookings Institution.

EIA (Energy Information Administration). 2003. *International Energy Outlook 2003*. Washington: US Department of Energy.

EIA (Energy Information Administration). 2006. *Annual Energy Outlook 2006*. Washington: US Department of Energy.

EIA (Energy Information Administration). 2007. *Annual Energy Outlook 2007*. Washington: US Department of Energy.

EIA (Energy Information Administration). 2008a. *International Energy Outlook 2008*. Washington: US Department of Energy.

EIA (Energy Information Administration). 2008b. *Annual Energy Outlook 2008*. Washington: US Department of Energy. Available at www.eia.gov/oiaf/archive/aeo08/index.html.

EIA (Energy Information Administration). 2010a. International Energy Statistics. Washington: US Department of Energy.

EIA (Energy Information Administration). 2010b. *Annual Energy Outlook 2010*. Washington: US Department of Energy.

EIA (Energy Information Administration). 2011a. *Electric Power Annual 2010*. Washington: US Department of Energy.

EIA (Energy Information Administration). 2011b. *Petroleum Supply Annual*. Washington: US Department of Energy.

EIA (Energy Information Administration). 2011c. *Review of Emerging Resources: US Shale Gas and Shale Oil Plays*. Washington: US Department of Energy.

EIA (Energy Information Administration). 2011d. *World Shale Gas Resources : An Initial Assessment of 14 Regions Outside the United States*. Washington: US Department of Energy.

EIA (Energy Information Administration). 2011e. *Model Documentation Report: Macroeconomic Activity Module (MAM) of the National Energy Modeling System*, volume 065. Washington: US Department of Energy.

EIA (Energy Information Administration). 2012a. *US Crude Oil, Natural Gas, and NG Liquids Proved Reserves*. Washington: US Department of Energy.

EIA (Energy Information Administration). 2012b. *Annual Energy Review* (September) Washington: US Department of Energy. Available at www.eia.gov/totalenergy/data/annual/index.cfm (accessed on September 8, 2013).

EIA (Energy Information Administration). 2012c. *Annual Energy Outlook 2012*. Washington: US Department of Energy.

EIA (Energy Information Administration). 2012d. *Effect of Increased Natural Gas Exports on Domestic Energy Markets*. Washington: US Department of Energy.

EIA (Energy Information Administration). 2012e. State Energy Data System. Washington: US Department of Energy

EIA (Energy Information Administration). 2013a. *Petroleum Supply Monthly*. Washington. Available at www.eia.gov/petroleum/supply/monthly.

EIA (Energy Information Administration). 2013b. Natural Gas Data. Washington: US Department of Energy.

EIA (Energy Information Administration). 2013c. International Energy Statistics. Washington: US Department of Energy.

EIA (Energy Information Administration). 2013d. *Monthly Energy Review*. Washington: US Department of Energy.

EIA (Energy Information Administration). 2013e. *Annual Energy Outlook 2013*. Washington: US Department of Energy

EIA (Energy Information Administration). 2013f. *Manufacturing Energy Consumption Survey 2010*. Washington: US Department of Energy.

EIA (Energy Information Administration). 2013g. *Petroleum & Other Liquids: Supply and Disposition*. Washington: US Department of Energy.

EPA (Environmental Protection Agency). 2010. *EPA Finalizes Regulations for the National Renewable Fuel Standard Program for 2010 and Beyond*. Washington.

EPA (Environmental Protection Agency). 2011a. *Investigation of Ground Water Contamination Near Pavillion, Wyoming*. Washington.

EPA (Environmental Protection Agency). 2011b. *EPA Finalizes 2011 Renewable Fuel Standards*, volume 211. Washington.

EPA (Environmental Protection Agency). 2012a. *EPA Finalizes 2012 Renewable Fuel Standards*, volume 211. Washington.

EPA (Environmental Protection Agency). 2012b. *EPA Finalizes 2013 Biomass-Based Diesel Volume*, volume 1. Washington: Environmental Protection Agency.

EPA (Environmental Protection Agency). 2012c. *National Emissions Inventory*. Washington.

EPA (Environmental Protection Agency). 2012d. Oil and Natural Gas Sector: New Source Performance Standards and National Emission Standards for Hazardous Air Pollutants Reviews; Final Rule. *Federal Register* 77, no. 159: 49490–600.

EPA (Environmental Protection Agency). 2013. *Inventory of US Greenhouse Gas Emissions and Sinks*. Washington.

EPA (Environmental Protection Agency) and Department of Transportation. 2012. 2017 and Later Model Year Light-Duty Vehicle Greenhouse Gas Emissions and Corporate Average Fuel Economy Standards. *Federal Register* 77, no. 199: 62624–63200.

ExxonMobil. 2013. *The Outlook for Energy: A View to 2040—US Edition*. Available at www.exxonmobil.com/Corporate/Files/news_pub_2013eo_us.pdf.

Gately, Dermot. 2007. What Oil Export Levels Should We Expect from OPEC ? *Energy Journal* 28, no. 2: 151–73.

Gately, Dermot, Hillard Huntington, John Mitchell, Mark Rodekohr, Mark Schwartz, and James Smith. 2004. OPEC's Incentives for Faster Output Growth. *Energy Journal* 25, no. 2: 75–96.

Gillingham, Kenneth, Matthew J. Kotchen, David S. Rapson, and Gernot Wagner. 2013. Energy Policy: The Rebound Effect Is Overplayed. *Nature* 493, no. 7433 (January 24): 475–76.

Goldberg, Linda S., and Keith Crockett. 1998. The Dollar and US Manufacturing. *Current Issues in Economics and Finance* 4 (November).

Goldman Sachs. 2010. *Commodity Prices and Volatility: Old Answers to New Questions*. New York.

Goldman Sachs. 2011. *Global Economics Weekly: A Tighter Oil Constraint—Less "Room to Grow."* New York.

Greene, David L., and Sanjana Ahmad. 2005. *Costs of U.S. Oil Dependence: 2005 Update*. Oak Ridge: Oak Ridge National Laboratory.

Hamilton, James D. 2009a. Causes and Consequences of the Oil Shock of 2007–08 Comments and Discussion. *Brookings Papers on Economic Activity* 2009, no. 1: 262–78.

Hamilton, James D. 2009b. Understanding Crude Oil Prices. *Energy Journal* 30, no. 2: 179–206.

Houser, Trevor. 2010. *Copenhagen, the Accord, and the Way Forward*. Policy Brief 10-5. Washington: Peterson Institute for International Economics.

Houser, Trevor. 2013. *Tracking America's Energy Bill*. New York: Rhodium Group.

Houser, Trevor, Shashank Mohan, and Ian Hoffman. 2010. *Assessing the American Power Act: The Economic, Employment, Energy Security, and Environmental Impact of Senator Kerry and Senator Lieberman's Discussion Draft*. Policy Brief 10-12. Washington: Peterson Institute for International Economics.

Howarth, Robert W., Renee Santoro, and Anthony Ingraffea. 2011. Methane and the Greenhouse-Gas Footprint of Natural Gas from Shale Formations. *Climatic Change* 106, no. 4 (April 12): 679–90.

Hufbauer, Gary Clyde, Allie E. Bagnall, and Julia Muir. 2013. *Liquefied Natural Gas Exports: An Opportunity for America*. Policy Brief 13-6. Washington: Peterson Institute for International Economics.

Huggett, Mark, and Gustavo Jaime Ventura. 1995. *Understanding Why High Income Households Save More Than Low Income Households*. Institute for Empirical Macroeconomics Discussion Paper 106. Federal Reserve Bank of Minneapolis.

IEA (International Energy Agency). 2002. *World Energy Outlook 2002*. Paris.

IEA (International Energy Agency). 2008. *World Energy Outlook 2008*. Paris.

IEA (International Energy Agency). 2010. World Oil Statistics. Paris.

IEA (International Energy Agency). 2011. *World Energy Outlook 2011*. Paris.

IEA (International Energy Agency). 2012a. *World Energy Outlook 2012*. Paris.

IEA (International Energy Agency). 2012b. *Medium-Term Gas Market Report 2012*. Paris.

IEA (International Energy Agency). 2012c. *Golden Rules for a Golden Age of Gas*. Paris: OECD Publishing.

IEA (International Energy Agency). 2013a. Monthly Oil Data Services. Paris.

IEA (International Energy Agency). 2013b. *Medium-Term Gas Market Report 2013*. Paris.

IHS CERA (Cambridge Energy Research Associates). 2012. *America's New Energy Future: The Unconventional Oil and Gas Revolution and the US Economy*, volume 1. Cambridge, MA.

IMF (International Monetary Fund). 2011. *World Economic Outlook: Tensions from the Two-Speed Recovery*. Washington.

IMF (International Monetary Fund). 2012. *International Financial Statistics*. Washington.

International E Chem. 2012. Petrochemicals Outlook. Presentation at the Citigroup investor conference, June 23.

International Gas Union. 2012. *World LNG Report 2011*. Fornebu, Norway.

IRS (Internal Revenue Service). 2010. *Table on Individual Income and Tax Data, by State and Size of Adjusted Gross Income*. Washington.

Jenkins, Jesse, Ted Nordhaus, and Michael Shellenberger. 2011. *Energy Emergence: Rebound and Backfire as Emergent Phenomena*. Oakland: Breakthrough Institute.

Jorgenson, Dale W., Mun Ho, and Jon Samuels. 2010. Information Technology and U.S. Productivity Growth: Evidence from a Prototype Industry Production Account. In *Industrial Productivity in Europe: Growth and Crisis*, ed. Matilde Mas and Robert Stehrer. Cheltenham: Edward Elgar Publishing.

JPMorgan. 2011. *US Equity Strategy Flash*. New York.

Juvekar, P. J., John J. Hirt, John K. Tysseland, and Sunil Sibal. 2012. *Cracker & Fracker Tour Takeaways: New Investments Invigorate US Gulf Coast*. New York: Citigroup.

Juvekar, P. J., and Faisel Khan. 2012. *US Ethylene Plants Getting Delayed as NGL Supply Surges Ahead: Ethylene Crackers Likely to Start Up Later Than Expected*. New York: Citigroup.

Killian, Lutz, and Bruce Hicks. 2013. Did Unexpectedly Strong Economic Growth Cause the Oil Price Shock of 2003-2008? *Journal of Forecasting* 32, no. 5: 385–94.

Koort, Robert, Brian Maguire, and Manav Gupta. 2012. *Riding a Wave of Ethane to an Ethylene Supercycle*. New York: Goldman Sachs.

Ladislaw, Sarah O., David Pumphrey, Frank A. Verrastro, Lisa A. Hyland, and Molly Walton. 2013. *Realizing the Potential of US Natural Gas*. Washington: Center for Strategic and International Studies.

Levi, Michael A. 2012a. Think Again: The American Energy Boom. *Foreign Policy* (July/August). Available at www.foreignpolicy.com/articles/2012/06/18/think_again_the_american_energy_boom.

Levi, Michael A. 2012b. *A Strategy for US Natural Gas Exports*. Washington: Brookings Institution.

Levi, Michael A. 2012c. Comment on "Hydrocarbon Emissions Characterization in the Colorado Front Range: A Pilot Study" by Gabrielle Pétron et al. *Journal of Geophysical Research: Atmospheres* 117, no. D21203 (November 16).

Levi, Michael A. 2013. *The Power Surge: Energy, Opportunity, and the Battle for America's Future.* Cambridge: Oxford University Press.

Lund, S., J. Manyika, S. Nyquist, L. Mendonca, and S. Ramaswamy. 2013. *Game changers: Five opportunities for US growth and renewal.* McKinsey Global Institute.

Macquarie. 2011. *US Economics Comment: Consumers Not Too Shocked about Oil.* New York.

Magud, Nicolás, and Sebastián Sosa. 2010. *When and Why Worry About Real Exchange Rate Appreciation? The Missing Link Between Dutch Disease and Growth.* IMF Working Paper WP/10/271. Washington: International Monetary Fund.

McKenzie, Lisa M., Roxana Z. Witter, Lee S. Newman, and John L. Adgate. 2012. Human Health Risk Assessment of Air Emissions from Development of Unconventional Natural Gas Resources. *Science of the Total Environment* 424: 79–87.

Medlock, Kenneth B. 2012. *US LNG Exports: Truth and Consequence.* Houston: James A. Baker III Institute for Public Policy, Rice University.

Montgomery, Carl T., and Michael B. Smith. 2010. Hydraulic Fracturing: History of an Enduring Technology. *Journal of Petroleum Technology* 62, no. 12: 26.

Morgan Stanley. 2011. *Oil Shock: A Mild Challenge to the Expansion.* New York.

Morse, Edward L., Eric G. Lee, Daniel P. Ahn, Aakash Doshi, Seth M. Kleinman, and Anthony Yuen. 2012. *Energy 2020: North America, the New Middle East?* New York: Citigroup.

Murti, Arun N., Matthew Carter-Tracy, and Dok Kwon. 2012. *Reasons to Remain Structurally Bullish: MidCon Refiners Increase.* New York: Goldman Sachs.

NBER (National Bureau of Economic Research). 2012. *US Business Cycle Expansions and Contractions.* Cambridge, MA. Available at www.nber.org/cycles/US_Business_Cycle_Expansions_and_Contractions_20120423.pdf.

NERA. 2012. *Macroeconomic Impacts of LNG Exports from the United States.* Washington: NERA Economic Consulting.

Nerurkar, Neelesh. 2012. *US Oil Imports and Exports: Policy.* Washington: Congressional Research Service.

NHTSA (National Highway Traffic Safety Administration). 2010. *Final Regulatory Impact Analysis: Corporate Average Fuel Economy for MY 2012–MY 2016 Passenger Cars and Light Trucks.* Washington: US Department of Transportation.

NPC (National Petroleum Council). 2007. *Facing Hard Truths.* Washington.

NPC (National Petroleum Council). 2011. *Prudent Development: Realizing the Potential of North America's Abundant Natural Gas and Oil Resources.* Washington.

NRC (National Research Council). 2009. *Hidden Costs of Energy: Unpriced Consequences of Energy Production and Use. Production.* Washington.

NRC (National Research Council), Committee on Induced Seismicity Potential in Energy Technologies, Committee on Earth Resources, Committee on Geological and Geotechnical Engineering, Committee on Seismology and Geodynamics, Board on Earth Sciences and Resources, and Division on Earth and Life Studies. 2012. *Induced Seismicity Potential in Energy Technologies.* Washington: National Academies Press.

Oil & Gas Journal. 2011. *OGJ Worldwide Refining Survey.* Tulsa, OK.

ORNL (Oak Ridge National Laboratory). 2012. *Transportation Energy Data Book.* Oak Ridge. Available at http://cta.ornl.gov/data/index.shtml.

Osborn, Stephen G., Avner Vengosh, Nathaniel R. Warner, and Robert B. Jackson. 2011. Methane Contamination of Drinking Water Accompanying Gas-well Drilling and Hydraulic Fracturing. *Proceedings of the National Academy of Sciences of the United States of America* 108, no. 20 (May 17): 8172–76.

Pétron, Gabrielle, Gregory Frost, Benjamin R. Miller, Adam I. Hirsch, Stephen A. Montzka, Anna Karion, Michael Trainer, Colm Sweeney, Arlyn E. Andrews, Lloyd Miller, Jonathan Kofler, Amnon Bar-Ilan, Ed J. Dlugokencky, Laura Patrick, Charles T. Moore Jr., Thomas B. Ryerson, Carolina Siso, William Kolodzey, Patricia M. Lang, Thomas Conway, Paul Novelli, Kenneth Masarie, Bradley Hall, Douglas Guenther, Duane Kitzis, John Miller, David Welsh, Dan Wolfe, William Neff, and Pieter Tans. 2012. Hydrocarbon Emissions Characterization in the Colorado Front Range: A Pilot Study. *Journal of Geophysical Research* 117, no. D04304 (February 21).

Pickering, Gordon. 2012. *North American Natural Gas Market Outlook, Fall 2012*. Chicago: Navigant Consulting, Inc.

PwC (PriceWaterhouseCoopers). 2011. *Shale gas: A renaissance in US manufacturing?* New York.

Rosen, Daniel H., and Trevor Houser. 2007. *China Energy: A Guide for the Perplexed*. Washington: Peterson Institute for International Economics and World Resources Institute.

Schurr, Sam H., and Bruce C. Netschert. 1960. *Energy in the American Economy, 1850–1975: An Economic Study of Its History and Prospects*. Baltimore, MD: Johns Hopkins Press.

Securing America's Future Energy. 2012. *The New American Oil Boom: Implications for Energy Security*. Washington.

Segall, Craig. 2012. *Look before the LNG Leap: Why Policymakers and the Public Need Fair Disclosure before Exports of Fracked Gas Start*. San Francisco: Sierra Club.

Selivanova, Julia. 2011. *Regulation of Energy in International Trade Law: WTO, NAFTA, and Energy Charter*. The Netherlands: Kluwer Law International.

Shellenberger, M., T. Nordhaus, A. Trembath, and J. Jenkins. 2012. *Where the Shale Gas Revolution Came From*. Oakland: Breakthrough Institute.

Stern, David I. 2011. The Role of Energy in Economic Growth. *Annals of the New York Academy of Sciences* 1219 (February): 26–51.

Trivedi, Kamakshya, Jose Ursua, George Cole, Julian Richers, and Dominic Wilson. 2012. *The Shale Revolution and the Global Economy*. New York: Goldman Sachs.

UNFCCC (United Nations Framework Convention on Climate Change). 2009. *Report of the Conference of the Parties on its Fifteenth Session, Held in Copenhagen from 7 to 19 December 2009: Addendum*. Geneva.

Verleger, Philip K. Jr. 2012. The Amazing Tale of US Energy Independence. *International Economy* (Spring). Available at www.international-economy.com/TIE_Sp12_Verleger.pdf.

Wang, Z., and A. Krupnick. 2013. *A Retrospective Review of Shale Gas Development in the United States: What Led to the Boom?* RFF Discussion Paper 13-12. Washington: Resources for the Future.

Wood Mackenzie. 2011. *US Supply Forecast and Potential Jobs and Economic Impacts*. Available at www.api.org/~/media/Files/Policy/Jobs/API-US_Supply_Economic_Forecast.pdf.

World Bank. 2013. *World Development Indicators*. Washington.

Yergin, Daniel. 1991. *The Prize: The Epic Quest for Oil, Money and Power*. New York: Simon & Schuster, Inc.

Yuen, Anthony, Seth M. Kleinman, Edward L. Morse, Eric G. Lee, Daniel P. Ahn, and Aakash Doshi. 2012. *Natural Gas: Bumpy Road to Global Markets Turbulence before the Golden Age and Competitive Markets*. New York: Citigroup.

Index

mercury, 101, 107, 111, 111f, 116, 145
methane, 4, 100, 114–15
Middle East, 1, 5–7, 48
Midwest states, 82, 97, 134, 144. *See also specific state*
Mineral Leasing Act of 1920, 133
Mississippi, 77, 79
Mitchell, George, 15, 93
Mitchell Energy, 15–16
monetary policy, 151–52
Montana, 20, 139–40
Monterey Formation (California), 20
motor vehicles
   energy efficiency, 1, 5–6, 67–72, 74, 156
   fuel costs, 46–47
multifactor productivity, 37

naphtha, 22, 74, 86–88, 91f
National Energy Modeling System (NEMS), 32–35, 42–46, 54, 68, 147–56
National Energy Technology Laboratory, 114
National Environmental Policy Act, 132, 140
National Highway Traffic Safety Administration (NHTSA), 67–68, 70, 156
National Oceanic and Atmospheric Administration (NOAA), 114–15
National Petroleum Council, 10–11
   energy production forecasts, 27t, 28f, 29f, 30–32
natural gas
   liquefied (*See* liquefied natural gas)
   shift from coal to, 100–101, 106–14, 117, 122, 133
Natural Gas Act of 1938, 125
natural gas exports, 3
   economic impact of, 129–32, 130t
   environmental issues, 132–33
   export applications, 125, 126t
   export capacity, 127–29, 128t
   GATT rules, 140–42
   trade policy and, 93, 123
natural gas imports
   forecasts, 32, 33f, 34f, 123–24, 124f
   as share of demand, 123–24, 124f
natural gas liquids (NGLs), 22, 74, 86–88
natural gas prices, 2
   versus alternative fuels, 88, 91f
   Asian growth and, 7–9, 8f
   demand and, 46
   economic cost of, 5–14
   exports and, 129–31, 130t
   versus oil prices, 19f, 20–22, 45f, 45–46, 47t
   supply constraints and, 10

supply surge and, 16, 17f, 19f, 46
   trade policy and, 93
natural gas production
   drilling activity (*See* drilling activity)
   environmental issues (*See* environmental issues)
   forecasts, 11, 12f, 24–32, 26f, 29f
   fugitive emissions, 114–15
   versus oil production, 20, 21f
   R&D programs, 15–16
   regional, 75–98, 144 (*See also* petrostates; *specific location*)
   reserves, 16, 18f
   technological advances, 2, 15–16, 22
natural gas supply
   constraints on, 10–11, 24
   economic impact of (*See* macroeconomic analysis)
   forecasts, 24, 27t
   surge in, 15–35
natural gas transmission and distribution module (NGTDM), 148
Nelson complexity index, 134, 134t
NEMS (National Energy Modeling System), 32–35, 42–46, 54, 68, 147–56
NERA Economic Consulting, 125, 129, 131
net export orientation, 93–94
Netherlands, 56–60
New Mexico, 20, 77, 97, 134
New York state, 30, 82
NGLs (natural gas liquids), 22, 74, 86–88
nitrogen oxide, 101–102, 107, 111, 111f, 116, 145
Nixon, Richard, 5
North American Free Trade Agreement (NAFTA), 133
North American pipeline network, 16, 135–38
North Dakota
   as petrostate, 75–82, 97, 144
   tight oil production in, 20–22, 134–35
North Sea, 47, 56–60
nuclear energy, 46, 108–11, 156

Obama, Barack, 2, 13–14
Ohio, 20
oil demand, 1, 65–74
   after global financial crisis, 11–14
   Asian growth and, 6–9, 7f
   changes in, 67, 68f
   consumption expenditures, 61–63, 63f
   exports and, 133
   fuel switching and, 72–74
   prices and, 46
   regional differences in, 95–96, 96f

Other Publications from the
Peterson Institute for International Economics

WORKING PAPERS

* = out of print

POLICY ANALYSES IN INTERNATIONAL ECONOMICS Series

Korea-United States Cooperation in the New
World Order*   C. Fred Bergsten and
Il SaKong, eds.
February 1996   ISBN 0-88132-226-1
Why Exports Really Matter!*
                         ISBN 0-88132-221-0
Why Exports Matter More!* ISBN 0-88132-229-6
J. David Richardson and Karin Rindal
July 1995; February 1996
Global Corporations and National Governments
Edward M. Graham
May 1996   ISBN 0-88132-111-7
Global Economic Leadership and the Group of
Seven   C. Fred Bergsten and C. Randall Henning
May 1996   ISBN 0-88132-218-0
The Trading System after the Uruguay Round*
John Whalley and Colleen Hamilton
July 1996   ISBN 0-88132-131-1
Private Capital Flows to Emerging Markets after
the Mexican Crisis*   Guillermo A. Calvo, Morris
Goldstein, and Eduard Hochreiter
September 1996   ISBN 0-88132-232-6
The Crawling Band as an Exchange Rate
Regime: Lessons from Chile, Colombia, and
Israel   John Williamson
September 1996   ISBN 0-88132-231-8
Flying High: Liberalizing Civil Aviation in the
Asia Pacific*   Gary Clyde Hufbauer and
Christopher Findlay
November 1996   ISBN 0-88132-227-X
Measuring the Costs of Visible Protection
in Korea*   Namdoo Kim
November 1996   ISBN 0-88132-236-9
The World Trading System: Challenges Ahead
Jeffrey J. Schott
December 1996   ISBN 0-88132-235-0
Has Globalization Gone Too Far?   Dani Rodrik
March 1997   ISBN paper 0-88132-241-5
Korea-United States Economic Relationship*
C. Fred Bergsten and Il SaKong, eds.
March 1997   ISBN 0-88132-240-7
Summitry in the Americas: A Progress Report
Richard E. Feinberg
April 1997   ISBN 0-88132-242-3
Corruption and the Global Economy
Kimberly Ann Elliott
June 1997   ISBN 0-88132-233-4
Regional Trading Blocs in the World Economic
System   Jeffrey A. Frankel
October 1997   ISBN 0-88132-202-4
Sustaining the Asia Pacific Miracle:
Environmental Protection and Economic
Integration   Andre Dua and Daniel C. Esty
October 1997   ISBN 0-88132-250-4
Trade and Income Distribution
William R. Cline
November 1997   ISBN 0-88132-216-4
Global Competition Policy   Edward M. Graham
and J. David Richardson
December 1997   ISBN 0-88132-166-4
Unfinished Business: Telecommunications after
the Uruguay Round   Gary Clyde Hufbauer and
Erika Wada
December 1997   ISBN 0-88132-257-1

Financial Services Liberalization in the WTO
Wendy Dobson and Pierre Jacquet
June 1998   ISBN 0-88132-254-7
Restoring Japan's Economic Growth
Adam S. Posen
September 1998   ISBN 0-88132-262-8
Measuring the Costs of Protection in China
Zhang Shuguang, Zhang Yansheng, and Wan
Zhongxin
November 1998   ISBN 0-88132-247-4
Foreign Direct Investment and Development:
The New Policy Agenda for Developing
Countries and Economies in Transition
Theodore H. Moran
December 1998   ISBN 0-88132-258-X
Behind the Open Door: Foreign Enterprises
in the Chinese Marketplace   Daniel H. Rosen
January 1999   ISBN 0-88132-263-6
Toward A New International Financial
Architecture: A Practical Post-Asia Agenda
Barry Eichengreen
February 1999   ISBN 0-88132-270-9
Is the U.S. Trade Deficit Sustainable?
Catherine L. Mann
September 1999   ISBN 0-88132-265-2
Safeguarding Prosperity in a Global Financial
System: The Future International Financial
Architecture, Independent Task Force Report
Sponsored by the Council on Foreign Relations
Morris Goldstein, Project Director
October 1999   ISBN 0-88132-287-3
Avoiding the Apocalypse: The Future of the
Two Koreas   Marcus Noland
June 2000   ISBN 0-88132-278-4
Assessing Financial Vulnerability: An Early
Warning System for Emerging Markets
Morris Goldstein, Graciela Kaminsky, and
Carmen Reinhart
June 2000   ISBN 0-88132-237-7
Global Electronic Commerce: A Policy Primer
Catherine L. Mann, Sue E. Eckert, and Sarah
Cleeland Knight
July 2000   ISBN 0-88132-274-1
The WTO after Seattle   Jeffrey J. Schott, ed.
July 2000   ISBN 0-88132-290-3
Intellectual Property Rights in the Global
Economy   Keith E. Maskus
August 2000   ISBN 0-88132-282-2
The Political Economy of the Asian Financial
Crisis   Stephan Haggard
August 2000   ISBN 0-88132-283-0
Transforming Foreign Aid: United States
Assistance in the 21st Century   Carol Lancaster
August 2000   ISBN 0-88132-291-1
Fighting the Wrong Enemy: Antiglobal Activists
and Multinational Enterprises
Edward M. Graham
September 2000   ISBN 0-88132-272-5
Globalization and the Perceptions of American
Workers   Kenneth Scheve and
Matthew J. Slaughter
March 2001   ISBN 0-88132-295-4
World Capital Markets: Challenge to the G-10
Wendy Dobson and Gary Clyde Hufbauer,
assisted by Hyun Koo Cho
May 2001   ISBN 0-88132-301-2

DISTRIBUTORS OUTSIDE THE UNITED STATES

Australia, New Zealand,
and Papua New Guinea
D. A. Information Services
648 Whitehorse Road
Mitcham, Victoria 3132, Australia
Tel: 61-3-9210-7777
Fax: 61-3-9210-7788
Email: service@dadirect.com.au
www.dadirect.com.au

India, Bangladesh, Nepal, and Sri Lanka
Viva Books Private Limited
Mr. Vinod Vasishtha
4737/23 Ansari Road
Daryaganj, New Delhi 110002
India
Tel. 91-11-4224-2200
Fax: 91-11-4224-2240
Email: viva@vivagroupindia.net
www.vivagroupindia.com

Mexico, Central America, South America,
and Puerto Rico
US PubRep, Inc.
311 Dean Drive
Rockville, MD 20851
Tel: 301-838-9276
Fax: 301-838-9278
Email: c.falk@ieee.org

Asia (*Brunei, Burma, Cambodia, China,*
Hong Kong, Indonesia, Korea, Laos, Malaysia,
Philippines, Singapore, Taiwan, Thailand,
and Vietnam)
East-West Export Books (EWEB)
University of Hawaii Press
2840 Kolowalu Street
Honolulu, Hawaii 96822-1888
Tel: 808-956-8830
Fax: 808-988-6052
Email: eweb@hawaii.edu

Canada
Renouf Bookstore
5369 Canotek Road, Unit 1
Ottawa, Ontario KlJ 9J3, Canada
Tel: 613-745-2665
Fax: 613-745-7660
www.renoufbooks.com

Japan
United Publishers Services Ltd.
1-32-5, Higashi-shinagawa
Shinagawa-ku, Tokyo 140-0002
Japan
Tel: 81-3-5479-7251
Fax: 81-3-5479-7307
Email: purchasing@ups.co.jp
For trade accounts only. Individuals will find
Institute books in leading Tokyo bookstores.

Middle East
MERIC
2 Bahgat Ali Street, El Masry Towers
Tower D, Apt. 24
Zamalek, Cairo
Egypt
Tel. 20-2-7633824
Fax: 20-2-7369355
Email: mahmoud_fouda@mericonline.com
www.mericonline.com

United Kingdom, Europe
(*including Russia and Turkey*)**, Africa,**
and Israel
The Eurospan Group
c/o Turpin Distribution
Pegasus Drive
Stratton Business Park
Biggleswade, Bedfordshire
SG18 8TQ
United Kingdom
Tel: 44 (0) 1767-604972
Fax: 44 (0) 1767-601640
Email: eurospan@turpin-distribution.com
www.eurospangroup.com/bookstore

Visit our website at:
www.piie.com
E-mail orders to:
petersonmail@presswarehouse.com